school success
for kids with
Autism

school success
for kids with
Autism

Edited by

Andrew L. Egel, Ph.D.,
Katherine C. Holman, Ph.D., CCC-SLP, &
Christine H. Barthold, Ph.D., BCBA-D

PRUFROCK PRESS INC.
WACO, TEXAS

Library of Congress Cataloging-in-Publication Data

School success for kids with autism / edited by Andrew L. Egel, Katherine C. Holman and Christine Hoffner.
     p. cm.
  ISBN 978-1-59363-746-0 (pbk.)
  1. Autistic children--Education. 2. Autistic children--Education--United States. 3. Autistic youth--Education--United States. 4. Inclusive education--United States. I. Egel, Andrew L., 1954- II. Holman, Katherine C., 1973- III. Hoffner, Christine, 1973-
  LC4718.S35 2012
  371.94--dc23
                        2011039305

Copyright © 2012 Prufrock Press Inc.
Edited by Lacy Compton
Cover Design by Raquel Trevino
Layout Design by Marjorie Parker

ISBN-13: 978-1-59363-746-0

At the time of this book's publication, all facts and figures cited are the most current available. All telephone numbers, addresses, and website URLs are accurate and active. All publications, organizations, websites, and other resources exist as described in the book, and all have been verified. The authors and Prufrock Press Inc. make no warranty or guarantee concerning the information and materials given out by organizations or content found at websites, and we are not responsible for any changes that occur after this book's publication. If you find an error, please contact Prufrock Press Inc.

Prufrock Press Inc.
P.O. Box 8813
Waco, TX 76714-8813
Phone: (800) 998-2208
Fax: (800) 240-0333
http://www.prufrock.com

Contents

Acknowledgements

I would like to thank my wife, Gina, for her support throughout this process; Lacy Compton for her careful reading and thoughtful comments; and Juli Katon for helping us ensure that the references for each chapter were complete. I especially want to thank the children with ASD and their families and teachers who have taught me so much about what is required to develop successful programs in schools, homes, and communities.—A. L. E.

I would first like to acknowledge my family for their unending support throughout this process, particularly my husband, Dusky, for his thoughtful edits and belief in me and this project. Thank you to Betsy Neville for her time and sincere encouragement. And last, but certainly not least, I am sincerely grateful to the children with ASD and their families, who have trusted in me and provided the amazing opportunity to work and learn from them in such a meaningful way.—K. C. H.

To my husband Ralph, who read drafts and provided feedback and, most importantly, support throughout the process. I would also like to acknowledge the children and adults with ASD who I serve and who challenge my assumptions every day.—C. H. B.

Introduction

Sara G. Egorin-Hooper

A true friend knows your weaknesses but
shows you your strengths; feels your fears but
fortifies your faith; sees your anxieties but
frees your spirit; recognizes your disabilities
but emphasizes your possibilities.

William Arthur Ward

IMAGINE your favorite friends coming over to spend the day to share adventure, food, and fun. You begin to think about your friends' interests, foods they love, and meaningful ways you can connect with them. You want to be respectful of and sensitive to each friend's unique interests and needs. You know that one friend has several food allergies that will require some planning and creative cooking. Some of your friends are active and love to hike while others tire more easily and enjoy hanging out. These individual differences comprise the mixed group of friends who will soon

1

be a special part of your planned day. You want to accommodate individually as well as collectively.

In preparing for their arrival, you think about what your friends will enjoy doing and set up the day based on what you know about them. You make a variety of dishes so there are some yummy choices for all. *You would never think of saying, "Well, this is all I made to eat, so it's too bad that you can't eat what's here; you'll just have to watch the rest of us while we eat."* After lunch, you choose a walking path, one with benches, so anyone can stop and pause during the walk if needed. *You would never say to your friend, "I'm sorry you're so wiped out—hang in there, we only have 5 more miles to go."* Clearly, what sensitive, caring people *intentionally* do is consider the interests, capabilities, and needs of those with whom they will be sharing time and space.

These are some of the considerations for creating a successful classroom experience for students with an autism spectrum disorder (ASD). Today's classrooms are made up of a very diverse group of students and each student has his own learning style. The student with an ASD brings his own unique learning strengths and challenges to a classroom, and there are both universal (meaning strategies that are helpful to *all* students) and ASD-specific strategies that can be put in place to ensure a positive and successful learning environment. This book will guide both educators and parents through these strategies across the age-span; however, despite the age of the student or the type of classroom, the fundamental component for success is the ability for teachers to create connections with and between their students.

Teachers are responsible for orchestrating meaningful relationships and learning in their classrooms each day. To accomplish this goal, teachers must demonstrate the willingness and open-mindedness to *see the value* of establishing an environment where their caring actions make a positive impact for students and *embrace the opportunity* to create an energizing classroom where all students belong and are invited to feel that their unique gifts are recognized and celebrated.

Creating an Inviting Classroom Community

Every day in a classroom needs to be like preparing for a visit from favorite friends. Just as you sustain your friends and are in turn sustained by them, the same dynamic exists between a teacher and her students. Teachers must also make the effort to create a memorable and mutually worthwhile classroom experience for all. Students and their families need to feel a sense of belonging from the moment they walk into the school.

Universal Educators

Every human being who touches the student's life is to be viewed as a "universal educator," including families who are integral and must be valued for their connection to and understanding of the whole student. Universal educators live and foster the message that we are "all students and teachers to each other," and learning is about taking in and making sense of experiences wherever we are and with whomever we are in life.

- The best universal educators don't see disability as a deficit, but rather as a difference. They use these differences as tools to motivate, teach, support, and actively engage each student in learning.

- The best universal educators model sincere, genuine appreciation and acknowledgment of each individual with whom they work, and then act intentionally to put purposeful strategies and supports in place.

- The best universal educators provide opportunities for students to contribute to the whole class—rather than always being the ones who are helped.

- The best universal educators respect, acknowledge, and consider ways to make learning accessible to students through choices that empower students, contribute to their success, and encourage them to take risks.

- The best universal educators, regardless of their title or role, continually reflect upon these qualities and imagine the possibilities that can and do result for students when meaningful, relevant classroom and instructional considerations are in place.

Thinking into the past to reflect on a favorite teacher conjures up first and foremost a memorable person who made us feel welcomed and valued in so many ways and modeled the real three Rs: relationships, respect, and relevance (not your grandmother's readin', writin', and 'rithmetic). Imagine a teacher who did this for you.

Relationships: Building Connections With Students

You are likely thinking of a teacher who learned your name right away and made you feel special by this personal acknowledgment; asked about personal experiences in your life such as your birthday party or how you were feeling when you returned from being absent from school; sent home a newsletter that included highlights of your daily activities and your accomplishments and acknowledged that you were part of a family; put up a bulletin board of photos of himself and other staff members along with a list of their favorite things; allowed students to have a bulletin board that did the same to give you something personal and tangible with which to connect; and met you at the door every day to greet you with a smile and a spirit of excitement about you being there and what you would learn that day, which made you want to come to school.

Respect: Fostering Mutual Trust

You are likely thinking of a teacher who recognized your keen interests or passions by complimenting you to others in the class and allowing you to share your ideas and stories; displayed everybody's artwork in the room and hallways and saw special talents in your artistic efforts, regardless of their lack of museum quality; gave you jobs so you could contribute to the class in a meaningful way and feel needed; invited others to your classroom so you could showcase your accomplishments and talents; and responded patiently to a wrong answer or off-beat question with "That's an interesting, creative way to look at that!" or "I've never thought of it in that way before."

Relevance: Showing Usefulness in What Is Learned

You are likely thinking of a teacher who gave you choices in your activities and assignments and showed he valued your opinions, ideas, and interests; allowed you to dance the "longitude and latitude" song, measure square footage going toe to heel as you walked across the floor, or learn addition and subtraction by hopping and jumping on the walk-on number line as fun, helpful ways to learn, practice, and understand something new and difficult; and gave you opportunities to get comfy in a beanbag or rocking chair, blow bubbles and catch them before they hit the ground, make favorite creatures out of play-dough, watch the fish swim in the classroom aquarium, or read a book outside in the courtyard on a nice spring day when you just needed time to be yourself and unwind.

Reframing Our Picture (the **Fourth R—** *One More for Good Measure!): Seeing Students From a Different Angle, Focusing on Students' Gifts, Strengths, Capabilities, and Possibilities Rather Than on Their Deficits and Limitations*

You are likely thinking of a teacher who always modeled forgiveness and recovered quickly even when upset with you; took the time to teach you positive, more socially acceptable ways to deal with your frustration, confusion, or social "misreads" and guided you in developing skills for handling difficult situations; let you know that if you could just get through a specific amount of work you thought was really hard, you could celebrate by having a set period of time to play your favorite computer game or read your favorite book; challenged you to expand your interests and exposed you to new learning when you insisted on staying with the one activity you liked; helped you save face when you rigidly dug in your heels; and addressed your need for structured and clear expectations by reminding you through chanting "and that's the rule in school."

All of these qualities contribute to the building of an authentic connection between students, families, and educators. These connections, these relationships are the foundation for successful learning in any classroom. Throughout this book, the reader will gain information on how to create a classroom environment that is nurturing, supportive, and effective for students with ASD, from early childhood through the transitioning adult. Parents will gain valuable information about what essential elements to look for in a classroom to successfully support their child with ASD. The intention is to provide useful details about curriculum content, instructional strategies and supports, and inclusion practices that are critical components in any classroom for a student with ASD. However, the reality lies in the true appreciation of starting with the information in this introduction: the importance of establishing meaningful relationships.

chapter 1

Introduction to Autism Spectrum Disorders

Andrew L. Egel

Have you ever been at sea in a dense fog, when it seemed as if a tangible white darkness shut you in and the great ship, tense and anxious, groped her way toward the shore with plummet and sounding-line, and you waited with beating heart for something to happen? I was like that ship before my education began, only I was without compass or sounding line, and no way of knowing how near the harbor was. "Light! Give me light!" was the wordless cry of my soul, and the light of love shone on me in that very hour.

Helen Keller

AUTISM was first described as a distinct clinical syndrome by Dr. Leo Kanner (1943). In his seminal study, Kanner described 11 patients whose symptoms he viewed as qualitatively different from anything that had been reported previously. Kanner noted that they all did not emotionally connect with others in their environment and did not exhibit affect under circumstances when it would have been appropriate. He described his patients' speech as atypical (e.g., pronoun reversals) and wrote that they obsessively insisted that their routines be followed exactly as they occurred previously. Kanner reported that his patients had a fascination with manipulating objects and appeared to be intelligent.

These characteristics have been revised and broadened over the past 50 years, with the most recent diagnostic criteria those in the *Diagnostic and Statistical Manual of Mental Disorders* (DSM-IV-TR) published by the American Psychiatric Association (2000). The DSM-IV-TR classifies Autistic Disorder (also referred to as autism), Pervasive Developmental Disorder–Not Otherwise Specified (PDD-NOS), Asperger's Disorder (also referred to as Asperger's syndrome), Rett's Disorder (also referred to as Rett's syndrome) and Childhood Disintegrative Disorder under the umbrella term *Pervasive Developmental Disorders*, often referred to as autism spectrum disorders (ASD). The specific characteristics listed in the DSM-IV-TR for Autistic Disorder are described in Figure 1.1 and a more detailed description of diagnostic/classification procedures are presented in Chapter 2.

A diagnosis of ASD is made using the DSM-IV-TR when an individual is qualitatively impaired in social interaction and communication and also exhibits patterns of behavior that are "restrictive, repetitive, and stereotyped" (APA, 2000, p. 71). Those diagnosed with ASD using the DSM-IV-TR represent a group of individuals with tremendous heterogeneity. For example, the majority of individuals with ASD will have some intellectual disability (formerly called mental retardation), although there are also individuals with the diagnosis who function in some areas at levels similar to typical peers. Similarly, some individuals with ASD may be nonverbal although others have expressive language that they use to control their environment. Despite the heterogeneity, each individual will have to meet the core characteristics outlined in the DSM-IV-TR in order to receive a diagnosis of ASD.

A. A total of six (or more) items from (1), (2), and (3), with at least two from (1), and one each from (2) and (3):

1. qualitative impairment in social interaction, as manifested by at least two of the following:
    a. marked impairment in the use of multiple nonverbal behaviors such as eye-to-eye gaze, facial expression, body postures, and gestures to regulate social interaction
    b. failure to develop peer relationships appropriate to developmental level
    c. a lack of spontaneous seeking to share enjoyment, interests, or achievements with other people (e.g., by a lack of showing, bringing, or pointing out objects of interest)
    d. lack of social or emotional reciprocity

2. qualitative impairments in communication as manifested by at least one of the following:
    a. delay in, or total lack of, the development of spoken language (not accompanied by an attempt to compensate through alternative modes of communication such as gesture or mime)
    b. in individuals with adequate speech, marked impairment in the ability to initiate or sustain a conversation with others
    c. stereotyped and repetitive use of language or idiosyncratic language
    d. lack of varied, spontaneous make-believe play or social imitative play appropriate to developmental level

3. restricted repetitive and stereotyped patterns of behavior, interests, and activities, as manifested by at least one of the following:
    a. encompassing preoccupation with one or more stereotyped and restricted patterns of interest that is abnormal either in intensity or focus
    b. apparently inflexible adherence to specific, nonfunctional routines or rituals
    c. stereotyped and repetitive motor mannerisms (e.g., hand or finger flapping or twisting, or complex whole-body movements)
    d. persistent preoccupation with parts of objects

B. Delays or abnormal functioning in at least one of the following areas, with onset prior to age 3 years: (1) social interaction, (2) language as used in social communication, or (3) symbolic or imaginative play.

C. The disturbance is not better accounted for by Rett's Disorder or Childhood Disintegrative Disorder.

Figure 1.1. Diagnostic criteria for Autistic Disorder.

Reprinted with permission from the *Diagnostic and Statistical Manual of Mental Disorders*, Fourth Edition, Text Revision, (Copyright© 2000). American Psychological Association.

Incidence

Evidence shows that boys are 3–4 times more likely than girls to be affected by autism. In addition, there is a greater likelihood that ASD will reoccur in the siblings of a child with a diagnosis of ASD (Ozonoff et al., 2011). This rate of reoccurrence is much higher than in the general population. We also know that children from all socio-economic levels and cultures can be diagnosed with ASD.

The overall occurrence of autism in the general population was initially identified as approximately 1 in 2,500 births. The Centers for Disease Control and Prevention (CDC; 2010), reporting on surveillance data from 2006, noted that the occurrence of autism spectrum disorders is now 1 in 110 births. This is a startling and substantial increase. Furthermore, it was also noted in the report that there was not one issue in particular that could explain the increase. For example, the CDC pointed out that no patterns were observed that would suggest that the increase in occurrence was attributable to the use of the broader ASD spectrum per se.

Etiology

Many potential causes of ASD have been discussed over the past decades (e.g., genetic/neurological/biochemical differences, deficiencies in the immune system, gastrointestinal problems, abnormal levels of neurotransmitters, environmental issues, poor parenting). The exact cause of ASD is unknown at the present time. There is a general consensus, however, that ASD is a neurodevelopmental disorder that may be influenced by a variety of factors (Sigman, Spence, & Wang, 2006). For example, several sources of evidence support the notion that genetics plays a role in the development of ASD. Studies have shown that if one identical twin has ASD, then there is a 60% chance that the other twin will also have ASD. The evidence also demonstrates that there is a 90% chance that the other twin will fall somewhere on the ASD spectrum even if he or she does not develop ASD[1] (Rutter, 2005). Evidence for a genetic component is also provided in research on non-twin siblings of children with ASD. These studies have shown that more than 10% of siblings of children with ASD are likely to exhibit deficits consistent with ASD (Boutot & Smith Myles, 2011). Although the above research is suggestive of a genetic link, additional evidence is clearly needed before any definitive conclusions can be reached.

There is also evidence to suggest that there may be structural differences in the brain of children with ASD when compared to typical peers. Some researchers have noted that the brains of children with ASD grow more rapidly than those of their typical peers (e.g., Courchesne et al., 2001). The rapid growth appears to affect specific areas of the brain that might make it difficult for children with ASD to interact with the environment during infancy.

The work in this area is fascinating, although it has not provided any definitive answers to the etiology of ASD. One should not expect that research in these areas will provide a "magic bullet" that will "cure" ASD, especially given the heterogeneity of people with ASD. Lord and Bishop (2010) noted that, despite the absence of a single, clear causal variable, individuals with ASD are all characterized by a specific set of social and communicative behavior problems that clearly distinguishes them from individuals with other diagnoses.

Social Characteristics of Individuals With ASD

Social deficits are one of the defining characteristics of ASD. As with other aspects of ASD, impairments in the area of social interaction can vary greatly from child to child. Deficits in this area are well documented in the literature and have been central to virtually all diagnostic criteria (e.g., DSM-IV-TR, National Society for Autistic Children

---

1   The fact that the rate of autism in identical twins is not 100% suggests that factors in addition to genetics are having an effect.

definition of the syndrome of Autism, Diagnostic Criteria for Autism Disorder [ICD-10]). The importance of these social deficits can also be seen by the tremendous amount of research that has been conducted to develop and evaluate interventions for increasing the social behavior of individuals with ASD (e.g., Reichow & Volkmar, 2010).

The social deficits characteristic of children with ASD are often seen very early in life. Parents of children with ASD have reported that their children did not respond to efforts to gain their attention and rarely made eye contact or attempted to obtain the attention of others through gestures or vocalizations (Thompson, 2007). Recent research has demonstrated that deficits in joint attention may be one of the earliest signs of social problems in very young children with ASD (e.g., Mundy & Burnette, 2005). Joint attention refers to a child's alternating attention between an object and a communication partner. Children display joint attention skills by initiating to others to pay attention to what they are attending to and by responding to another person's cues (e.g., pointing) to attend to a particular stimulus or set of stimuli in which the partner is interested. Joint attention skills are critical because, with typical children, they are highly correlated with early acquisition of receptive and expressive language as well as other, more complex skills. Several authors (e.g., Jones & Carr, 2004; Kasari, Freeman, & Paparella, 2001, 2006; Landa, Holman, O'Neill, & Stuart, 2011; Martins & Harris, 2006; Whalen, Schreibman, & Ingersoll, 2006) have suggested that the deficit in joint attention behaviors should be a high priority for intervention because their absence may be related to the core problems in social and communicative behavior.

Social deficits continue to be evident as children with ASD grow older. Teachers and parents may notice that children with ASD do not develop friendships (e.g., not initiating contact with peers or respond-ing when peers initiate contact with them) that are appropriate for their age. Similar problems can be seen even with children with ASD whose skills are more advanced. For example, such individuals may have more difficulty negotiating social situations because they do not understand the rules governing social interactions. Finally, the social deficits can also be seen in the children's play skills. Children with

ASD do not typically initiate play with other students, or engage in pretend or imaginative play. Their play is often characterized as being very repetitive or only showing interest in parts of a toy (e.g., spinning the wheels of a car).

Communication Characteristics of Individuals With ASD

As noted previously, both receptive and expressive communication are usually very impaired in individuals with ASD. Deficits in language comprehension include the inability to understand simple directions, questions, or instructions. Some individuals may be nonverbal while others have some language but do not use it for social communication. Individuals with ASD who do speak may engage in echolalia, which is the immediate or delayed repetition of words or phrases that they have heard previously. Several researchers (e.g., Prizant & Duchan, 1981; Prizant & Rydell, 1984; Schreibman & Carr, 1978) demonstrated that immediate and delayed echolalia may have different functions. For example, a student with ASD might use an echolalic response to indicate affirmation, make a request, or as a response to incomprehensibility.

Even if echolalia is not present, the communication deficits often prevent individuals with ASD from initiating or participating in reciprocal conversation. Such problems may be compounded because people with ASD often exhibit a literal understanding of what is being said, but have difficulties responding appropriately to the nuances of language. For example, a teacher may tell a student with ASD to "move it" in an effort to get the student to transition more quickly. The student, however, may respond by actually moving an item from one location to another. Individuals with ASD also have difficulty communicating nonverbally, such as through hand gestures, eye contact, and facial expressions.

Repetitive and Stereotypical Behaviors

Several behaviors identified in the DSM-IV-TR are part of the autism diagnostic criteria that often interfere with effective presentation of instruction. Many individuals with ASD exhibit stereotypic behaviors such as body rocking, spinning objects or themselves, hand flapping, and repetitive vocalizations. These behaviors are often maintained by the sensory consequences that are produced (e.g., visual, auditory, tactile, vestibular); however, they may also enable a person to avoid or delay an unpleasant event (e.g., instruction; Kennedy, Meyer, Knowles, & Shukla, 2000). It is also common for individuals with ASD to engage in ritualistic behaviors that can impact instruction. For example, they may repetitively line up materials in the exact same manner or show distress if the same schedule is not followed day to day. Tantrums and noncompliance may occur frequently, although such behaviors are not unique to individuals with ASD.

Asperger's Syndrome

Asperger's syndrome (AS) was first described by Hans Asperger in 1944. Individuals with AS share many characteristics with those diagnosed as having autism, but there are also some clear differences. For example, individuals with either diagnosis have "qualitative impairments in social interaction" and "restricted repetitive and stereotyped patterns of behavior, interests, and activities" (APA, 2000, pp. 75, 84). However, the language and cognitive impairments characteristic of those with autism are not present in individuals with AS. Figure 1.2 shows the characteristics for AS, as outlined by the DSM-IV-TR.

Although the language of persons with AS is not technically delayed, their pragmatic communication abilities are typically affected. This is especially evident when using language in a social context. For example, conversations with typical peers are often very one-sided because individuals with AS will perseverate on topics that are of

A. Qualitative impairment in social interaction, as manifested by at least two of the following:
   1. marked impairment in the use of multiple nonverbal behaviors such as eye-to-eye gaze, facial expression, body postures, and gestures to regulate social interaction
   2. failure to develop peer relationships appropriate to developmental level
   3. a lack of spontaneous seeking to share enjoyment, interests, or achievements with other people (e.g., by a lack of showing, bringing, or pointing out objects of interest to other people)
   4. lack of social or emotional reciprocity

B. Restricted repetitive and stereotyped patterns of behavior, interests, and activities, as manifested by at least one of the following:
   1. encompassing preoccupation with one or more stereotyped and restricted patterns of interest that is abnormal either in intensity or focus
   2. apparently inflexible adherence to specific, nonfunctional routines or rituals
   3. stereotyped and repetitive motor mannerisms (e.g., hand or finger flapping or twisting, or complex whole-body movements)
   4. persistent preoccupation with parts of objects

C. The disturbance causes clinically significant impairment in social, occupational, or other important areas of functioning.
D. There is no clinically significant general delay in language (e.g., single words used by age 2 years, communicative phrases used by age 3 years).
E. There is no clinically significant delay in cognitive development or in the development of age-appropriate self-help skills, adaptive behavior (other than in social interaction), and curiosity about the environment in childhood.
F. Criteria are not met for another specific Pervasive Developmental Disorder or Schizophrenia.

Figure 1.2. Diagnostic criteria for Asperger's syndrome.

Reprinted with permission from the *Diagnostic and Statistical Manual of Mental Disorders*, Fourth Edition, Text Revision, (Copyright© 2000). American Psychological Association.

interest to them even though the particular topic is not interesting to peers. As a result, further attempts to communicate may not be reciprocated by peers. Many individuals with AS also speak very formally to their peers while showing a lack of formality when communicating with adults. Individuals with AS also have difficulty with nonverbal social communication. For example, people with AS may stand too close to the person with whom they are interacting, potentially creating an uncomfortable situation that might reduce future interactions. People with AS sometimes have difficulties understanding gestures or facial expressions and, as a result, may fail to comprehend communication that occurs within an interaction. The above issues often create problems in establishing more typical, age-appropriate friendships. However, unlike individuals with autism, those with AS may be interested in developing friendships but do not have the understanding of social roles that enable them to establish and sustain friendships (Simpson & Smith Myles, 2011).

Conclusion

ASD is a disorder that affects 1 in 110 children. The tremendous behavioral heterogeneity of individuals with ASD, both in terms of severity of behaviors and skills, can make instructional programming difficult. The following chapters will identify what we know about instructional programming for students with ASD at the preschool, elementary, and secondary levels and how such environments can be established so that learning can be maximized.

References

American Psychiatric Association. (2000). *Diagnostic and statistical manual of mental disorders* (4th ed., Text Rev.). Washington, DC: Author.

Boutot, E. A., & Smith Myles, B. (2011). *Autism spectrum disorders: Foundations, characteristics, and effective strategies.* Upper Saddle River, NJ: Pearson.

Centers for Disease Control and Prevention. (2010). *Autism and developmen-*

tal disabilities monitoring (ADDM) network. Retrieved from http://www. cdc.gov/ncbddd/autism/addm.html

Courchesne, E., Karnes, C. M., Davis, H. R., Ziccardi, R., Carper, R. A., . . . Courchesne, R. A. (2001). Unusual brain growth in early life in patients with autistic disorder: An MRI Study. *Neurology, 57,* 245–254.

Jones, E. A., & Carr, E. G. (2004). Joint attention in children with autism: Theory and intervention. *Focus on Autism and Other Developmental Disabilities, 19,* 13–16.

Kanner, L. (1943). Autistic disturbances of affective contact. *Nervous Child, 2,* 217–253.

Kasari, C., Freeman, S., & Paparella, T. (2001). Early intervention in autism: Joint attention and symbolic play. *International Review of Research in Mental Retardation, 23,* 207–237.

Kasari, C., Freeman, S., & Paparella, T. (2006). Joint attention and symbolic play in young children with autism: A randomized controlled intervention study. *Journal of Child Psychology and Psychiatry, 47,* 611–620.

Kennedy, C. H., Meyer, K. A., Knowles, T., & Shukla, S. (2000). Analyzing the multiple functions of stereotypical behavior for students with autism: Implications for assessment and treatment. *Journal of Applied Behavior Analysis, 33,* 559–571.

Landa, R. J., Holman, K. C., O'Neill, A. H., & Stuart, E. A. (2011). Intervention targeting development of socially synchronous engagement in toddlers with autism spectrum disorders: A randomized controlled trial. *Journal of Child Psychology and Psychiatry, 52,* 13–21.

Lord, C., & Bishop, S. L. (2010). Autism spectrum disorders: Diagnosis, prevalence, and services for children and families. *Social Policy Report, 24,* 1–21.

Martins, M. P., & Harris, S. L. (2006). Teaching children with autism to respond to joint attention initiations. *Child & Family Behavior Therapy, 28,* 51–68.

Mundy, P., & Burnette, C. (2005). Joint attention and neurodevelopmental models of autism. In F. R. Volkmar, R. Paul, A. Klin, & D. Cohen (Eds.), *Handbook of autism and pervasive developmental disorders: Diagnosis, development, neurobiology, and behavior* (pp. 650–681). Hoboken, NJ: Wiley.

Ozonoff, S., Young, G. S., Carter, A., Messinger, D., Yirmiya, N., Zwaigenbaum, L., . . . Stone, W. L. (2011). Recurrence risk for autism spectrum disorders: A baby siblings research consortium study. Pediatrics, *128*, e488–e495.

Prizant, B. M., & Duchan, J. F. (1981). The functions of immediate echolalia in autistic children. *Journal of Speech and Hearing Disorders, 46,* 241–249.

Prizant, B. M., & Rydell, P. J. (1984). Analysis of functions of delayed echolalia in autistic children. *Journal of Speech and Hearing Research, 27,* 183–192.

Reichow, B., & Volkmar, F. R. (2010). Social skills interventions for individuals with autism: Evaluation for evidence-based practices within a best evidence synthesis framework. *Journal of Autism & Developmental Disorders, 40,* 149–166.

Rutter, M. (2005). Autism research: Lessons from the past and prospects for the future. *Journal of Autism & Developmental Disorders, 35,* 241–257.

Schreibman, L., & Carr, E. G. (1978). Elimination of echolalic responding to questions through the training of a generalized verbal response. *Journal of Applied Behavior Analysis, 11,* 453–463.

Sigman, M., Spence, S. J., & Wang A. T. (2006). Autism from developmental and neuropsychological perspectives. *Annual Review of Clinical Psychology, 2,* 327–355.

Simpson, R. L., & Smith Myles, B. (2011). *Asperger syndrome and high functioning autism: A guide for effective practice* (3rd ed.). Austin, TX: PRO-ED.

Thompson, T. (2007). *Making sense of autism.* Baltimore, MD: Brookes.

Whalen, C., Schreibman, L., & Ingersoll, B. (2006). The collateral effects of joint attention training on social initiations, positive affect, imitation, and spontaneous speech for young children with autism. *Journal of Autism & Developmental Disorders, 36,* 655–664.

chapter 2

Assessment of Students With Autism Spectrum Disorders in the School Setting

April J. Schwarz

> You cannot help men permanently by doing for them what they could do for themselves.
>
> Abraham Lincoln

AUTISM has become an area of intense focus in the past 10 years. As noted in Chapter 1, this disorder, once considered rare, is reportedly now occurring in as many as one in 110 children (Centers for Disease Control and Prevention [CDC], 2010). Equally astonishing, the number of students with ASD served under the Individuals with Disabilities Education Improvement Act (IDEA) has increased by more than 500% (U.S. Government Accountability Office, 2005). Speculation regarding the increase includes improved identification practices, broadening criteria, and a combination of environmental and genetic/medical causes (Wing & Potter, 2009). Regardless of the potential causes or reasons, it is crucial for parents and school personnel to become familiar with specific ASD characteristics and assessment procedures, because early identification and intervention tend to produce better outcomes (e.g., Brock, Jimerson, & Hansen, 2006; Coonrod & Stone, 2005). Assessment is also crucial to understanding which interventions should be in place at the various school levels.

Classic autism symptoms can sometimes be identified in a child as early as 12–18 months of age (Coonrod & Stone, 2005). Between 2 and 3 years old, diagnosis becomes more reliable. Still, the CDC reports the median age range of earliest ASD diagnosis as 3 years, 5 months to 5 years, 7 months (Rice, 2009). Children who display mild characteristics tend to be identified later than children who present with classic autism features. Accordingly, some students will enter the school system already having an initial ASD diagnosis, while others will not. Therefore, school personnel and parents will increasingly be expected to participate in the identification, assessment, and education of students with ASD.

The increased focus on ASD has also encouraged development of various diagnostic and assessment tools. As students with ASD demonstrate a varied profile of strengths and weaknesses, assessment has sometimes proven to be challenging. However, with more assessment tools being designed with specific ASD characteristics in mind, developing a profile of a student's unique strengths and weaknesses is more tangible. As a result, better-targeted interventions, strategies, and accommodations can be developed.

ASD encompasses a complex range of skills and abilities, best described by Klin (2009) as follows:

> individuals with PDD range from those who are profoundly intellectually disabled to those with IQs in the gifted range; from those who are non-verbal to those who are hyper verbal; from those who are extraordinarily socially isolated to those who cannot stop themselves from approaching others, albeit inappropriately and from those whose lives are enchained by stereotypic movements or repetitive behaviors to those whose lives are dominated by learning about unusual topics. (p. 91)

Therefore, a comprehensive assessment that evaluates this wide range of strengths and weaknesses is understandably vital and necessary.

Purpose of Assessment

The purposes of assessment change over the course of a student's life and educational experience (Shea & Mesibov, 2009). The initial purposes of a school assessment are twofold: (1) to determine the presenting issues (i.e., diagnosis), and (2) to determine educational impact and eligibility for special education services as defined by IDEA. This means moving beyond a diagnosis and identifying how the student's learning is affected by the disability that was found. Although DSM-IV-TR (American Psychiatric Association [APA], 2000) criteria are referenced, educational eligibility is defined by federal regulations. Autism is one of 15 IDEA eligibility categories for special education. Specifically, IDEA (2004) defines autism as

> a disability significantly affecting the child's verbal and nonverbal communication and social interaction, generally evident before age 3 years, that adversely affects his or her educational performance. Other characteristics often associated with autism are engagement in repetitive activities and stereotyped movements, resistance to environmental change or change in daily routines, and unusual responses to sensory experiences. Autism does not apply if a child's educational performance is adversely affected primarily because the child has an emotional disturbance. A child who manifests the characteristics of autism after age 3 years could be identified as having autism if he or she has the characteristic symptoms. (Part 300/A/300.8)

The IDEA autism criteria are a broad definition such that IDEA should include most students with an ASD. However, determining eligibility and educational impact becomes more difficult when assessing students on the milder end of the spectrum. Thus, a comprehensive assessment becomes even more crucial in order to identify those specific social communication deficits and the extent to which the student's functioning is affected. It is important to remember the school system's focus is to determine eligibility within the criteria of the IDEA categories. Eligibility is not based upon a medical diagnosis. A medical diagnosis of an ASD is not a requirement for a school team to determine educational eligibility but, in many cases, is information a school team would review and consider when conducting a comprehensive evaluation.

One of the most important purposes of assessment is to craft a unique profile of learning strengths and weaknesses, which in turn will inform targeted interventions. Klin, Saulnier, Tsatsanis, and Volkmar (2005) discussed the importance of identifying the oftentimes "scattered" profile of students with ASD, and the need for a skilled multidisciplinary or transdisciplinary team of professionals to have experience with a wide range of ASD characteristics in order for splinter skills to be interpreted in the right context. The assessment information gathered, more importantly, will help all involved gain a perspective about the student's strengths and needs that will enable them to better identify supports and help plan for the future. In later years, a reevaluation may be required in order to reconfirm eligibility. However, once ASD is documented, reevaluation progresses to a periodic measurement, evaluation, and benchmarking of progress toward all goals, with the ultimate goal of independence. Furthermore, once the student is middle to high school age, assessment purposes shift toward transition planning for life after school (e.g., adult services, vocational training, higher educational opportunities).

Considerations/Preparation for Assessment

Preparation for assessment, as well as the structure of the testing environment, is an important part of the assessment process. This is due to the inherent difficulties students with ASD tend to exhibit (i.e., inflexibility, need for sameness or cognitive rigidity, anxiety, lack of social reciprocity, attention and motivation difficulties; Koegel, Koegel, & Smith, 1997). In fact, Koegel et al. (1997) demonstrated improvements in IQ testing when reinforcement procedures (e.g., providing access to highly motivating activities contingent upon on task responding; see Chapter 3 for more details on reinforcement) and individualized strategies (e.g., scheduling frequent breaks, permitting the student to sit on the floor, having a parent accompany the child to the testing session) were implemented to increase attention and motivation. It is incumbent upon the examiner to gather information from parents/caregivers and teachers prior to testing the student, to be able to implement and structure as positive a testing environment as possible. In doing so, results will less likely be based on compliance and motivation of the student (Koegel et al., 1997). The following suggestions are by no means meant to be used as a checklist for every student, because each student will vary widely in his needs. However, appropriate consideration is needed regarding how these areas affect a student's ability to participate in a testing situation.

Recognition that students with ASD often display variable behavior, motivation, and attention from day to day requires the examiner to be flexible in planning, thinking, and execution of the assessment. Flexibility applies to every aspect; for instance, being willing to test on a different day than originally planned, providing frequent breaks, and testing in smaller segments over a period of several days.

Parents/caregivers and teachers can provide critical information regarding what motivates a student, what reinforcers he likes, and what interests and activities he enjoys. This information is central to structuring the testing environment, as the goal is to make this time as highly rewarding/reinforcing as possible for the student. This information can be obtained by simply asking parents and teachers what they have observed, by observing the student in his natural environment and noting what he is drawn to, or by asking parents and teachers to complete a quick reinforcer/preference assessment. Noting the type of self-stimulatory behavior present can also provide a clue to the student's interests (i.e., does he tend to like toys that make sounds or does he gravitate toward objects he can squeeze in his hand?). Providing access to these items and using them as motivation for on-task behavior will most likely increase motivation, attention, and compliance (Koegel et al., 1997).

Some students with ASD have difficulty transitioning to new or unfamiliar environments and people. In effect, they have difficulty with change in their routine. The examiner should carefully consider the place, time, and whether a staff member is necessary during the evaluation. For instance, if the testing room is unfamiliar to the student, familiarize him with the room by allowing several visits prior to the day of formal evaluation. Providing access to a preferred activity while visiting will also help ease his anxiety and reinforce a positive experience. Likewise, if the examiner is unknown to the student, extra time should be spent letting the student become familiar with the examiner. This is the perfect opportunity to work with the student in an unthreatening manner, pairing yourself with reinforcement. Utilization of a different room that is more familiar to the student (such as his classroom when other students are not there) might be another option. If the student is very reluctant to change, letting him remain at his desk might reduce some anxiety. Additionally, the presence of a staff member who is close to the student or the parent (for very young children) might be considered necessary to help deliver reinforcement or provide comfort if the student is experiencing excessive anxiety or noncompliance. The individual is not, however, to administer or give clues to any part of the test.

Visual schedules, token systems, and use of timers have also been helpful in increasing compliance and reducing anxiety in students with ASD. A visual schedule can assist a student by helping him see and understand how long the session will last and what tasks need to be completed. Use of a "First-Then" schedule, where a picture of a task is placed under First and a picture of the earned reward is placed under Then, is an example of a differentiated visual strategy to help the student understand what to do and expect. None of these interfere with test administration protocol. A deviation from the administration protocol, or from how the test was supposed to be given, would mean that the test is no longer considered standardized, thus resulting in answers that cannot be scored. It is important to administer a test consistently, *the way it was standardized*, so that the results are valid, interpretable, and can be compared to norms (i.e., same-aged peers, same grade-level peers).

The way in which the student communicates is also important to know. How does the student make her basic needs and wants known? What is the mode of communication used by the student? If the student is nonverbal, are pictures, signs, or gestures used to let you know if the student needs water, wants a break, or needs to use the bathroom? Scheduling frequent breaks involving sensory strategies such as jumping, walking around the building, or accessing sensory objects (e.g., stress balls) will allow the student some time to decompress without actually having to request an opportunity for a break.

Lastly, the physical environment can be easily adapted to suit the student's needs. Some examples are making sure the table and chair are size appropriate, utilizing a chair that doesn't swivel or move (this can become highly distracting for the student), covering up or taking down distracting objects in the room, positioning one side of the testing table against the wall, and positioning oneself differently (i.e., behind or next to instead of across from the student) to be close enough to deliver reinforcement quickly when needed (Brock et al., 2006).

Ozonoff, Goodlin-Jones, and Solomon (2005) suggested that if an examiner has a wide range of experience and understanding of ASD symptoms, then few students would be "untestable." In other words, more students would be able to take a standardized test and meaningful information could be collected and compared to group data. However, even with ample preparation for a testing session, there will likely be a handful of students who still cannot take a standardized assessment for a wide range of reasons (e.g., difficulty sitting, attending to directions, engaging in high rates of self-stimulatory behavior, difficulty with pointing). In such situations, the educational team would then rely on anecdotal information or information gathered from giving a test in a nonstandardized way. This is why planning for the aforementioned difficulties beforehand will potentially increase the likelihood of a more engaging, motivating, and meaningful assessment process.

Components of a Comprehensive Evaluation

A comprehensive evaluation typically entails a multimethod approach, which involves obtaining feedback from several sources (e.g., parents, teachers, students), by utilizing multiple assessment techniques (e.g., interview, observation, standardized and informal testing measures). Pertaining specifically to assessment of ASD, the literature suggests evaluation of core domains, although no specified battery of tests for autism is suggested. Recommended assessments include taking a detailed developmental history (via interview with parents/caregiver), behavioral observations across different settings/environments, and measurement of intellectual ability, adaptive behavior, social skills, and language/communication skills (Ozonoff et al., 2005). Within the school setting, academic functioning would be a necessary domain to assess as well. Still other areas of functioning may need to be evaluated depending upon the specific needs of the student (i.e., fine motor skills, executive functioning skills). Once those needs are identified as areas of concern, any combination of professionals—speech therapists, occupational therapists, special education teachers, general education teachers, and/or school psychologists—would constitute the school evaluation team.

There are numerous assessment tools available to measure functioning across these domains. Consequently, only a few of the more well-known scales can be highlighted. In addition, there are various rating tools specific to ASD that have been developed. The scales summarized in Table 2.1 were chosen based on the frequency with which these scales have been used in research. This is not to say, however, that scales not summarized in this table do not have utility.

In addition, there are various rating tools specific to ASD that have been developed. Rating scales are important in the evaluation process

Table 2.1

Summary of ASD Instruments

Assessment Tool	Age Range	Number of Items	Administration Time	Purpose
Autism Diagnostic Interview Revised (ADI-R)	2+	93	Up to 3 hours	Parent/caregiver interview Targets ASD characteristics and developmental milestones Provides diagnostic information
Autism Diagnostic Observation Schedule (ADOS)	Sections based on language level	4 sections	30–45 min. each section	Semistructured observational tool Assessment of play and communication skills Provides diagnostic information
Childhood Autism Rating Scale–Second Edition (CARS-2)	2+	15	Varies depending on observation	Observational tool completed by professionals High-functioning version and parent questionnaire available Targets specific ASD characteristics Measures severity of ASD
Social Communication Questionnaire (SCQ)	4+	40	5–10 min.	Parent questionnaire with yes/no format Targets specific ASD characteristics Screening measurement provides diagnostic information
Social Responsiveness Scale (SRS)	4–18 years	65	15 min.	Parent and teacher forms Targets ASD characteristics Screening tool; measures severity of social impairment

as they gather data from multiple sources regarding behavior in different environments. However, rating scales are subject to some bias, such as the rater's perceptions, stress, and motivation for assessment. Additionally, most of the autism-specific rating scales continue to have a range of difficulties (Naglieri & Chambers, 2009). One concern raised is the question of the rating scale's validity, that is, does the scale actually measure what it says it measures? Still another concern is whether the results will be the same over time, referring to its reliability. Although highly utilized within the school setting, caution is needed when over-reliance on these scales, or the scores they produce, seems evident. Meaning, in effect, that clinical judgment is necessary to carefully analyze, synthesize, and interpret data from all sources to ultimately formulate a diagnosis or an eligibility reason for special education services.

To that end, two specific tools: (1) the Autism Diagnostic Interview-Revised (ADI-R; Rutter, LeCouteur, & Lord, 2003), and (2) the Autism Diagnostic Observation Schedule (ADOS; Lord, Rutter, DiLavore, & Risi, 1999) will be reviewed later in this chapter because their diagnostic and assessment utility is indicated in ASD research. When administered in combination, they are often considered the "gold standard" of diagnosis and assessment of ASD. However, use of these specific tools is not commonplace in the school setting primarily because of the amount of training, expense, and time required for administration and scoring. Despite this fact, school personnel are routinely asked to review private, outside evaluations in which these tools have been used and, therefore, it is important to be informed about them.

Suggested Assessment Domains

Interview/Developmental History

A thorough developmental history is usually the first step in an initial assessment. The information gathered from an interview with parents/caregivers is used to formulate a picture of the developing child and aids in differential diagnosis. Information needs to be gained regarding the attainment of developmental milestones (e.g., social, communication, motor, play/joint attention), prenatal and birth history, medical history (including hearing and vision screening), family history of developmental disabilities and/or other psychiatric disabilities, and noted areas of strength, concern, and interest.

This information can be gathered by an informal interview or by use of structured instruments. There are many developmental questionnaires that are used in general such as the Ages and Stages Questionnaire (Bricker & Squires, 1994), Battelle Developmental Inventory (Newborg, 2004), Child Development Inventory (CDI; Ireton, 1992), and others. However, a critical component in the diagnosis of ASD relies heavily on gaining an accurate representation of skills and behaviors over time. Due to the highly variable nature of ASD behaviors (e.g., changes across setting and time, noted regressions), past behavioral information may not be uncovered when using a general developmental inventory. For that reason, the Autism Diagnostic Interview-Revised (ADI-R; Rutter, LeCouteur, et al., 2003) is examined below.

The ADI-R is a semistructured interview that systematically asks questions regarding developmental milestones, but at the same time focuses on behaviors that are indicative of a diagnosis of ASD. Unique questions range from topics about atypical language skills (e.g., loss of language skills, echolalia), socialization skills (e.g., use of social smiling and eye gaze, social interactions, play skills), to sensory interests and ritualistic and/or more idiosyncratic behaviors. The only requirement is the child must have a mental age of at least 2 years. The ADI-R has the ability to capture current behavior exhibited as well as behavior across the lifespan. Thus, this tool captures abnormalities that presented earlier in life. Administration can be long (up to 2 1/2 hours), and an ASD cut-off score is derived from algorithms, which can be arduous to score. In that respect, this tool is not frequently used in the school setting. However, it is understandable why the information gained from this interview is highly desirable when making an initial diagnosis. Therefore, early intervention services and preschool programs, which are typically attended around the age of initial referral, might be wise to consider the ADI-R as part of their assessment and interview process with parents.

How parents can use this information for their child. When parents are going through the initial eligibility process and thus participating in an interview about their child's developmental milestones and history, sometimes reviewing this information all at one time will help gain a more comprehensive picture of their child's development. The interviewer and parents may identify not only milestone achievements but also patterns of behavior and any atypical communication or socialization skills. Reviewing the child's history will most likely be the first step in deepening parents' understanding about their child's current skill level and diagnosis. Additionally, knowing patterns of behavior or atypical development of one child will always be beneficial to parents in identifying warning signs or similar patterns of behavior in the future, should they have additional children.

Behavioral Observation

Direct observation of the student is another critical area of assessment because it allows for observation of behavior free from the perceptions of others. School system personnel are in the unique position of being able to observe a student in a natural environment—the school setting. In effect, students should be observed when presented with the daily requirements of a social environment, both in structured (e.g., academic subjects/classroom) and nonstructured (e.g., recess, lunch) parts of the day. Observations within this context will provide information regarding how the student typically behaves, communicates, and interacts with others. This can aid in differential diagnosis of other disabilities as well as ASD. In fact, Goldstein, Ozonoff, Cook, and Clark (2009) recommended observation across many days and/or even weeks to be able to truly appreciate the range of ASD symptoms present. Although time is limited for school personnel, the opportunity to observe a student in a naturally social environment is a valuable component of school assessment. However, for students just turning school age or who have never attended school, home observations may be necessary to gain an understanding of the student's functioning in a familiar environment. In these situations, it is highly important for parents to share observations of their child, particularly with regard to the child's use of language, interaction with others, unusual interests or behaviors, and/ or any sensory sensitivity. Another situation that may necessitate home observations is when a student is reportedly demonstrating skills in one environment and not the other. This information would be useful in determining an intervention for generalizing the skill.

Observation of presently existing behaviors (e.g., stereotypical behaviors such as hand flapping, head banging, or echolalic speech), as well as behaviors lacking or absent (e.g., spoken language, initiation of interactions with others, eye contact), are both necessary and important. The school environment lends itself to observing a student's need and response to structure, how a student deals with change and transitions within a classroom or different classrooms, and the quality of communication, play, and social interactions such as initiating conversations with other children and social reciprocity skills. Atypical communication skills such as echolalia, repeating scripts from TV or the movies, pronoun reversals, or demonstrating voice modulation difficulty with volume, tone, and register may also be noted.

For higher functioning individuals, an observation during an academic period—especially if it is an area of chosen interest—may show the student's academic capabilities, but the social communication deficits might not always be clear. On the other hand, an observation during lunch, recess, or another unstructured period of time may highlight social deficits (e.g., initiating and maintaining conversations, whether a preference to be alone or take part in group activities is demonstrated, engagement in one-sided conversations). Behavioral excesses such as the flapping of hands/arms, jumping, or other stereotypic behaviors might also be more prevalent.

The gold standard observational tool used for diagnosis and assessment of ASD in research is the Autism Diagnostic Observation Schedule (ADOS; Lord et al., 1999). The ADOS is a semistructured, play-based assessment that allows the examiner to observe social communication and play skills. Four modules based on different levels of language skills and/or age can each take 45 minutes to administer. Most likely all four modules will not be administered. Although the first two modules focus on observing social communication within the context of play, the latter two modules use unstructured conversations and questions to examine social communication skills. Diagnosis is based on algorithms and cut-off scores are provided for the presence of autism and ASD in general. Although this tool is considered to be the most psychometrically sound observation tool in ASD research, its use is limited in the school setting due to the expense, training required, and the amount of time required for administration.

To summarize, direct observation of the student across multiple settings and time frames to observe social, communication, and behavioral excesses and deficits firsthand is critical in creating a profile of strengths and needs for the student. Direct observation in the home environment might also be necessary in certain circumstances (i.e., the student is very young, the student has never attended school, the student has divergent skill levels). This crucial information, along with the parent report, will assist in formulating targeted and attainable goals that focus on skill acquisition and generalization of that skill.

How parents can use this information for their child. Observations of a student by professionals will give parents a window of information and help them see how their child behaves and performs in novel situations and other social situations. Parents can use this information to understand what conditions, such as environmental cues or structure of setting, help or hinder their child's ability to demonstrate a specific skill. This, in turn, will assist parents in formulating a plan that will help their child use his skills in multiple environments.

Rating Scales Specific to ASD

The amount of specific ASD rating scales available has significantly increased over the past few years. These tools should be used to gather information regarding the student's functioning in different environments based upon ratings from multiple informants. Rating scales can typically be completed by anyone familiar with the student (e.g., teachers, parents/caregivers, outside therapists working with the student). Some common rating scales utilized in school settings include, but are not limited to, the Childhood Autism Rating Scale (CARS; Schopler, Reichler, & Renner, 1988), the Gilliam Autism Rating Scale–Second Edition (GARS-2; Gilliam, 2006), the Social Communication Questionnaire (SCQ; Rutter, LeCouteur, et al., 2003), and the Social Responsiveness Scale (SRS; Constantino & Gruber, 2005). Additionally, rating scales such as the Asperger Syndrome Diagnostic Scale (ASDS; Myles, Bock, & Simpson, 2001), Australian Scale for Asperger's Syndrome (ASAS; Attwood, 1998), and Gilliam Asperger's Disorder Scale (GADS; Gilliam, 2001) are common rating scales used when a student is suspected of having Asperger's syndrome. A brief review of selected rating scales follows. Although all rating scales have difficulties, as mentioned previously, these scales were selected for review due to their well-supported psychometric properties.

The Childhood Autism Rating Scale (Schopler et al., 1988) is an observational rating tool developed to help identify the severity of autistic symptoms and differentiate children with other developmental disorders. Fifteen skills are rated on a scale of 1 (*normal behavior*) to 4 (*severely abnormal functioning*) based upon an examiner's observation of the student or reported parental observations. The CARS results in a total score with cut-off score ranges that help differentiate symptoms of ASD. The recently published CARS-2 (Schopler, Van Bourgondien, Wellman, & Love, 2010) includes three forms: CARS-2 Standard Version (CARS-2 ST), CARS-2 High Functioning Version (CARS-2 HF), and a Questionnaire for Parents (CARS-2 QPC). Because the original CARS was once the most widely used and best-documented scale to measure autism, the CARS-2 ST retained the same familiar format with updated norms and items based on DSM-IV-TR criteria.

The Social Communication Questionnaire (SCQ; Rutter, Bailey, & Lord, 2003) is a rating scale based on selected questions from the ADI-R. In fact, it is a shortened version of the ADI-R. It is a parental rating form designed simply in a yes/no format, essentially differing from the ADI-R interview format. Accordingly, the SCQ also contains current and lifetime behavior forms with recommended cut-off scores indicating ASD and differentiates the various forms of ASD. It also requires the student to demonstrate a mental age of 2 years.

The Social Responsiveness Scale (SRS; Constantino & Gruber, 2005) is a questionnaire covering various dimensions of interpersonal behavior, communication, and repetitive/stereotypical behaviors indicative of ASDs. There are separate parent and teacher rating forms and an age range of 4–18 years old. This tool measures the severity of social reciprocity. This is one of the few scales for which standard scores are reported. The five subscales include: Social Awareness, Social Cognition, Social Communication, Social Motivation, and Autistic Mannerisms.

How parents can use this information for their child. Again, because the information gathered by a rating scale as a stand-alone instrument in general can be subject to bias, parents should not rely solely or separately on the information gathered. Rather, parents can use this information to aid in the understanding of how other professionals rated their child's functioning in comparison to students who have already been identified with an ASD. Specific ASD rating scales can also inform parents of the characteristics of ASD in general. Finally, the information gathered from a rating scale might be useful for future reference when a child undergoes reevaluation, especially if the same rating scale is completed by the same parent. It would provide comparison data of behaviors that were present previously compared to behaviors demonstrated currently. Such information would highlight potential progress if a behavior was no longer present or help identify patterns of behavior that were demonstrated consistently.

Intellectual Functioning

Intellectual functioning is an important area to assess, partly because it is one of the best predictors of future outcomes (Klinger, O'Kelley, & Mussey, 2009). In fact, intellectual disability rates for students with ASD vary widely, depending upon the specific diagnosis. For example, 40% to 71% of individuals diagnosed with autism have been reported to also have an intellectual disability, compared to 6% to 49% of individuals with a diagnosis of PDD-NOS (Klinger et al., 2009). Asperger's syndrome is not associated with an intellectual disability. IQ is also associated with gender difference (girls with autism tend to demonstrate lower IQ scores as compared to boys), medical conditions (seizure disorders are associated with lower IQ scores), and severity of autism symptoms, which are documented in a review of the literature by Ozonoff et al. (2005). As a result, many prominent ASD research-ers assert intellectual assessment is the "frame" for the observation and assessment findings of a student (Klin et al., 2005; Ozonoff et al., 2005). The purpose of intellectual assessment is not to obtain a score on a test, but rather understand how best a student learns to problem solve. Historically, an uneven cognitive profile has been reported for students with ASD. However, caution is recommended when interpreting "islets of information" because this information does not generalize to other areas of functioning (Klin ct al., 2005; Klinger et al., 2009). The authors use a clear example to highlight this point: "an average IQ score may overestimate ability in a child's weakest skills and underestimate ability in the child's strongest skills" (Klinger et al., 2009, p. 216). Although a specific test profile has not emerged, cognitive impairments in abstract and flexible thinking skills, as well as perspective taking skills have been noted. Students with ASD tend to focus on details, seeing the proverbial tree, but missing the forest. On the other hand, strengths have been documented in block design, musical skills, memory of specific facts, and calendar calculation (Klinger et al., 2009). Also, there is some evi-dence to suggest some students with Asperger's syndrome demonstrate higher scores on verbal IQ compared to performance IQ (Klin et al., 2005; Ozonoff et al., 2005).

Due to the wide range in cognitive ability, selecting an appropriate cognitive test is sometimes a difficult task. Klin et al. (2005) recom-mended these criteria for test selection to better meet the needs of the student: (1) level of language skills required, (2) the complexity of the instructions and the tasks, (3) the level of social demands, (4) the utilization of timed tasks, and (5) number of shifts from one subtest or format to another. For students who are on the mild side of the spectrum and who demonstrate verbal abilities, the common cognitive assessment measures such as the Wechsler scales (Wechsler, 2002, 2003) or the Stanford-Binet Intelligence Scales (SB5; Roid, 2003) are considered appropriate. Other verbal IQ tests that tend to be useful due to their wider age range are the Differential Abilities Scale–2 and the Kauffman Assessment Battery for Children–Second Edition (Klin et al., 2005; Ozonoff et al., 2005).

For students who are nonverbal and/or have lower mental ages, the Leiter International Performance Scale–Revised (Leiter-R; Roid & Miller, 1997) is the test of choice (Klin et al., 2005). There are two separate batteries: Visualization and Reasoning (VR) and Attention and Memory (AM). The VR measures nonverbal reasoning and visual-spatial skills. The age range is from 2 years to almost 21 years. Directions are delivered nonverbally, and the test allows for certain items to be modeled. It does not require use of any receptive or expressive language. Nevertheless, should this not be a feasible choice, several of the developmental scales such as the Bayley Scales of Infant and Toddler Development, Third Edition (Bayley, 2005) and the Mullen Scales of Early Learning (Mullen, 1995) may also be used.

How parents can use this information for their child. As stated earlier in the chapter, because cognitive ability has been proven to be one of the best predictors of future success, the information gathered provides a framework for parents in shaping and developing future plans and expectations. Cognitive assessment particularly helps parents understand how their child learns information and how they problem solve best. Most likely, some areas of strength as well as areas of weakness will be identified, which in turn can help parents understand how best to teach their child. Different information will be highlighted depending upon the cognitive assessment that was administered. For example, a verbal intelligence test such as the WISC-IV might provide insight into how visual motor processing and working memory affect a child's performance. Knowing that a child has difficulty with visual motor processing, for example, might lead to recommendations for accommodations on the IEP such as extended time, a scribe, or access to assistive technology devices. On the other hand, a test like the Leiter-R would inform parents if their child is able to solve unfamiliar visual-spatial tasks or whether the child's pure matching skills are a strength area. For example, using visual schedules and picture cues more frequently might help your child understand the world around him more fully if he has significant difficulty solving nonverbal problems, but demonstrates strengths on pure matching skills. Incidental information regarding how your child performed behaviorally during the testing session (e.g., how well he or she can transition from different tasks, topics, and nonpreferred activities) may also help formulate plans that parents can use to increase the flexibility of their child, starting in a safe environment such as the home.

Adaptive Behavior Functioning

Adaptive behavior is generally considered to be the performance of daily activities required for personal and social sufficiency (Sparrow, Cicchetti, & Balla, 2005). Measuring adaptive behavior determines how one functions in the world compared to his same-age peers and expectations. Specifically, it examines how much supervision or independence a student demonstrates in taking care of personal needs and managing community living. For students with ASD, this often is an area of great disability influenced by the amount of interfering behavior present and level of intellectual functioning. However, adaptive behavior is not static and changes over time. Therefore, assessment of adaptive behavior translates into highly individualized goals for a student's future. The measure of adaptive behavior is also necessary for classification of an intellectual disability. Furthermore, being able to compare and contrast parent and teacher ratings of daily functioning is crucial to understanding the conditions that support inconsistent demonstration and/or generalization of a skill (i.e., type of prompt, different expectations). For example, if a student is toilet trained at home but not at school, this skill would likely be targeted as a goal on the student's Individualized Education Program (IEP).

There are various adaptive behavior rating forms that can be completed by teachers and parents/caregivers. Although not a comprehensive list, some examples include the Vineland Adaptive Behavior Scales, Second Edition (Sparrow et al., 2005), Adaptive Behavior Scale–School, Second Edition (Lambert, Nihira, & Leland, 1993), and the Scales of Independent Behavior–Revised (SIB-R; Bruiniks, Woodcock, Weatherman, & Hill, 1996).

The first edition of the Vineland Adaptive Behavior Scales (Sparrow, Balla, & Cicchetti, 1984) is reported to be the most widespread measure of adaptive skills (Klin et al., 2005). This assesses functioning in communication, daily living skills, socialization skills, and motor skills for students 5 years old and younger. The second edition of these scales has three forms: a parent interview form, a parent rating form, and a teacher form. The updated version includes norms specific to individuals with autism and Asperger's syndrome.

How parents can use this information for their child. Measurement of a child's adaptive behavior is one of the areas that influences highly specific and targeted interventions. Therefore, information from adaptive rating scales will help parents gain a concrete understanding of their child's level of independent functioning for daily life skills. If adaptive rating scales are completed by more than one person in different environments, parents will have a better understanding of how skills are being generalized and/or transferring to other environments. This means that the parents will be able to identify the prompt level necessary for their child to produce a skill and will be able to recognize other environmental cues or structure support. This could easily be turned into a task analysis (i.e., the systematic breaking down of a skill into smaller steps) to help the child function more independently at home. Finally, the information gathered from adaptive rating scales can provide a nice benchmark of progress with each individual skill over time.

Communication/Language Functioning

Absence, delays in, or atypical use of language and communication skills are one of the key deficits in ASD. Consequently, it is important to have an accurate and comprehensive assessment of not only expressive and receptive language skills, but also an assessment of language comprehension and pragmatics. Depending on the language abilities of the student, informal assessment may be necessary rather than using standardized measures. Nonetheless, there are a variety of general instruments that are used to evaluate receptive and expressive language skills, such as the Peabody Picture Vocabulary Test, Fourth Edition (Dunn & Dunn, 2007), Expressive One-Word Picture Vocabulary Test–Fourth Edition (Martin & Brownell, 2010), Clinical Evaluation of Language Fundamentals–Preschool, Second Edition (Semel, Wiig, & Secord, 2004), and the Preschool Language Scale, Fourth Edition (Zimmerman, Steiner, & Pond, 2002).

For high-functioning students with ASD, an evaluation should also examine pragmatics, which is the use of language in social situations. Behaviors that might be assessed include nonverbal behaviors (e.g., eye contact, gestures, facial expressions, body language), turn taking, and understanding of inferences and figurative expressions. Some pragmatic language tests suggested by Paul (2005) include the Test of Language Competence (Wiig & Secord, 1989), the Children's Communication Checklist–2 (Bishop, 2006), and the Comprehensive Assessment of Spoken Language (Carrow-Woolfolk, 1999). A comprehensive evaluation that incorporates pragmatics is often most important to the student with Asperger's syndrome (AS). Students with AS typically demonstrate adequate receptive and expressive language skills. However, deficits are noted in pragmatic language, semantics, and language expression. For example, students with AS demonstrate difficulty modulating voice tone and volume, taking turns in conversations, and understanding nonliteral speech (such as humor) and others' emotions. Within the school setting, the speech-language pathologist would analyze the intricacies of the student's use of language to gain a thorough understanding of higher level language formation and conversational success as part of a comprehensive evaluation. Lastly, many children with ASD do not develop verbal language at all. For this reason, assessment for Augmentative or Alternative Communication (AAC) will be vital for establishing a way for the student to communicate her wants and needs. For some students who exhibit one- to two-word phrase speech, language samples can be collected to document and analyze mean utterance length, word use, and/or presence of other atypical language such as echolalia or pronoun reversals (Paul, 2005).

How parents can use this information for their child. Parents will gain valuable information regarding their child's ability to use and understand verbal and nonverbal language, language comprehension skills, and language processing abilities from a language assessment. This information will help guide parents in deciding the most productive way to teach their child (e.g., via verbal instruction, use of a Picture Exchange Communication System [PECS], or sign language; when there's a need for AAC devices). For parents who have children with higher levels of language and social skills, understanding their child's difficulties with social comprehension and social communication skills will help develop targeted interventions and goals within both the communication and social skills domains. This information will often help parents decide whether or not their child could benefit from a social skills group or other supports outside of the school setting.

Academic Functioning

Historically, assessing the academic levels of students with ASD has been difficult, particularly in students with classic autism. Currently, two assessment tools are available that target this population of students with ASD: the Psychoeducational Profile–Third Edition (PEP-3; Schopler, Lansing, Reichler, & Marcus, 2005) and the TEACCH Transition Assessment Profile, Second Edition (TTAP; Mesibov, Thomas, Chapman, & Schopler, 2007).

The PEP-3 (Schopler et al., 2005) is an assessment tool that measures cognitive and adaptive skills and behaviors typical of students with ASD and other developmental disabilities in order to plan educational goals. The testing age range is 6 months to 7 years old. It consists of direct testing and observation as well as a caregiver/parent report. Skills are rated as passing, emerging, or failing across several adaptive domains and as appropriate, mild, or severe on the maladaptive behavior abilities. It results in statistics such as percentile ranks and developmental levels that allow for comparison of the child with ASD to other students with ASD and/or a typical comparison group. The three main measured domains are Communication, Motor, and Maladaptive Behaviors.

The TTAP (Mesibov et al., 2007) focuses on functional areas that are necessary for transition planning for high-school-aged students with ASD. It consists of direct testing and observation in different environments such as school, work, and home or residential setting. The functional areas assessed include vocational skills, vocational behavior, independent functioning, leisure skills, functional communication, and interpersonal behavior. Skills are rated as passing, emerging, or failing.

For students who are higher functioning, standardized assessments as well as informal assessments are appropriate for use. Two examples of educational assessments frequently used are the Woodcock-Johnson III Tests of Cognitive Abilities (WJ-III; Woodcock, McGrew, & Mather, 2001) and the Wechsler Individual Achievement Test–Second Edition (WIAT-II; Wechsler, 2001).

How parents can use this information for their child. Assessing academic performance levels will give parents a general idea of how their child's knowledge compares with the levels achieved by their same-aged peers. This applies to students who are able to take assessments such as the WJ-III and WIAT-II. Specific academic strengths and weaknesses are identified and can be analyzed in terms of whether it is the content or the fluency of the student's learning that makes her excel or gives her difficulty. For children who are assessed by measures such as the PEP-3 and TTAP, data gathered from these scales can be used to generate specific goals. The added bonus of these instruments is that they provide the ability to track progress over time. For example, because these scales rate skills as passing, emerging, or failing, a parent can very easily track her child's progress across time with multiple administrations of these scales.

Other Areas of Functioning That Might Require Assessment

Additional areas of dysfunction have been reported in students with ASD. Depending on the specific needs of the student, different areas that may very possibly need to be evaluated include executive functioning skills (e.g., cognitive flexibility; the abilities to plan, inhibit behavior, organize, and self-monitor) together with attention deficits, social skills, and social-emotional functioning (to rule out other disorders such as ADHD, anxiety, or depression). Many of these skills are evaluated by parent and teacher reports on a multitude of rating scales. For the higher functioning individual, self-report measures are a unique way of assessing perceptions.

Conclusion

In summary, students with ASD are a growing population of children in the school setting. Assessment of ASD is complex and requires a multidisciplinary approach with well-trained professionals who have had a wide range of experience with ASD and are able to interpret the uneven profile of strengths and weaknesses by this student population. The purposes of assessment that vary across the student's age level were discussed, as well as the specific considerations for engaging and motivating students with ASD in the assessment process. Important components of an evaluation were reviewed, and core ASD domains for assessment were recommended. They included: a comprehensive developmental history (interview), behavioral observations across time and multiple settings, adaptive behavior, intellectual functioning, communication/language skills, and academic functioning. Selected tools within each of the core domains were reviewed, highlighting which were appropriate for use with students with ASD. The gold standard diagnosis and assessment tools in ASD research were also reviewed for a better understanding of their use.

In summary, there is no set battery of tests to assess students with ASD. Rather, an individualized approach based upon a student's unique characteristics should be considered when selecting appropriate measures. In doing so, the assessment process will be more reflective of a student's skill level, ultimately resulting in better crafted recommendations and interventions for the student's future.

References

American Psychiatric Association. (2000). *Diagnostic and statistical manual of mental disorders* (4th ed., Text Rev.). Washington, DC: Author.

Attwood, T. (1998). *Asperger's syndrome: A guide for parents and professionals.* London, England: Jessica Kingsley.

Bayley, N. (2005). *Manual for the Bayley Scales of Infant and Toddler Development* (3rd ed.). San Antonio, TX: Harcourt Assessment.

Bishop, D. (2006). *Children's Communication Checklist–2* (American Standardization Version). London, England: Harcourt Assessment.

Bricker, D., & Squires, J. (1994). *Ages and Stages Questionnaire.* Baltimore, MD: Brookes.

Brock, S. E., Jimerson, S. R., & Hansen, R. L. (2006). *Identifying, assessing, and treating autism at school.* New York, NY: Springer.

Bruiniks, R. H., Woodcock, R. W., Weatherman, R. F., & Hill, B. K. (1996). *Scales of Independent Behavior–Revised.* Chicago, IL: Riverside.

Carrow-Woolfolk, E. (1999). *Comprehensive Assessment of Spoken Language.* Circle Pines, MN: American Guidance Service.

Centers for Disease Control and Prevention. (2010). *Autism and developmental disabilities monitoring (ADDM) network.* Retrieved from http://www.cdc.gov/ncbddd/autism/addm.html

Constantino, J. N., & Gruber, C. P. (2005). *Social Responsiveness Scale.* Los Angeles, CA: Western Psychological Services.

Coonrod, E. E., & Stone, W. L. (2005). Screening for autism in young children. In F. R. Volkmar, R. Paul, A. Klin, & D. J. Cohen (Eds.),

Handbook of autism and pervasive developmental disorders (3rd ed., pp. 707–729). Hoboken, NJ: Wiley.

Dunn, L. M., & Dunn, D. M. (2007). *Peabody Picture Vocabulary Test* (4th ed.). Bloomington, MN: Pearson.

Gilliam, J. E. (2001). *Gilliam Asperger's Disorder Scale.* Austin, TX: PRO-ED.

Gilliam, J. E. (2006). *Gilliam Autism Rating Scale* (2nd ed.). Austin, TX: PRO-ED.

Goldstein, S., Ozonoff, S., Cook, A., & Clark, E. (2009). Alternative methods, challenging issues, and best practices in the assessment of autism spectrum disorders. In S. Goldstein, J. Naglieri, & S. Ozonoff (Eds.), *Assessment of autism spectrum disorders* (pp. 358–372). New York, NY: Guilford Press.

Individuals with Disabilities Education Improvement Act, Pub. Law 108-446 (December 3, 2004).

Ireton, H. (1992). *Child Development Inventory.* Minneapolis, MN: Behavior Science Systems.

Klin, A. (2009). Subtyping the autism spectrum disorders: Theoretical, research, and clinical considerations. In S. Goldstein, J. Naglieri, & S. Ozonoff (Eds.), *Assessment of autism spectrum disorders* (pp. 91–116). New York, NY: Guilford Press.

Klin, A., Saulnier, C., Tsatsanis, K., & Volkmar, F. R. (2005). Clinical evaluation in autism spectrum disorders: Psychological assessment within a transdisciplinary framework. In F. R. Volkmar, R. Paul, A. Klin, & D. J. Cohen (Eds.), *Handbook of autism and pervasive developmental disorders* (3rd ed., pp. 772–798). Hoboken, NJ: Wiley.

Klinger, L. K., O'Kelley, S. E., & Mussey, J. L. (2009). Assessment of intellectual functioning in autism spectrum disorders. In S. Goldstein, J. Naglieri, & S. Ozonoff (Eds.), *Assessment of autism spectrum disorders* (pp. 209–252). New York, NY: Guilford Press.

Koegel, L. K., Koegel, R. L., & Smith, A. (1997). Variables related to differences in standardized test outcomes for children with autism. *Journal of Autism and Developmental Disorders, 27,* 233–243.

Lambert, N., Nihira, K., & Leland, H. (1993). *Adaptive Behavior Scale— School* (2nd ed.). Austin, TX: PRO-ED.

Lord, C., Rutter, M., DiLavore, P. C., & Risi, S. (1999). *Autism Diagnostic Observation Schedule*. Los Angeles, CA: Western Psychological Services.

Martin, N. A., & Brownell, R. (2000). *Expressive One-Word Picture Vocabulary Test* (4th ed.). Novato, CA: Academic Therapy.

Mesibov, G., Thomas, J. B., Chapman, S. M., & Schopler, E. (2007). *TEACCH Transition Assessment Profile* (2nd ed.). Austin, TX: PRO-ED.

Mullen, E. M. (1995). *Mullen Scales of Early Learning*. Circle Pines, MN: American Guidance Service.

Myles, B. S., Bock, S. J., & Simpson, R. L. (2001). *Asperger Syndrome Diagnostic Scale*. Austin, TX: PRO-ED.

Naglieri, J. A., & Chambers, K. M. (2009). Psychometric issues and current scales for assessing autism spectrum disorders. In S. Goldstein, J. A. Naglieri, & S. Ozonoff (Eds.), *Assessment of autism spectrum disorders* (pp. 55–90). New York, NY: Guilford Press.

Newborg, J. (2004). *Battelle Developmental Inventory* (2nd ed.). Meadows, IL: Riverside.

Ozonoff, S., Goodlin-Jones, B., & Solomon, M. (2005). Evidence-based assessment of autism spectrum disorders in children and adolescents. *Journal of Clinical Child and Adolescent Psychology, 34*, 523–540.

Paul, R. (2005). Assessing communication in autism spectrum disorders. In F. R. Volkmar, R. Paul, A. Klin, & D. J. Cohen (Eds.), *Handbook of autism and pervasive developmental disorders* (3rd ed., pp. 799–816). Hoboken, NJ: Wiley.

Rice, C. (2009). Prevalence of autism spectrum disorders—Autism and developmental disabilities monitoring network, United States, 2006. *Morbidity and Mortality Weekly Report: Surveillance Summaries, 58*(SS10), 1–20.

Roid, G. H. (2003). *Stanford-Binet Intelligence Scales* (5th ed.). Chicago, IL: Riverside.

Roid, G. M., & Miller, L. J. (1997). *Leiter International Performance Scale–Revised: Examiner's Manual*. Wood Dale, IL: Stoelting.

Rutter, M., Bailey, A., & Lord, C. (2003). *Social Communication Questionnaire*. Los Angeles, CA: Western Psychological Services.

Rutter, M., LeCouteur, A., & Lord, C. (2003). *Autism Diagnostic Interview–Revised*. Los Angeles, CA: Western Psychological Services.

Schopler, E., Lansing, M. D., Reichler, R. J., & Marcus, L. M. (2005). *Psychoeducational Profile* (3rd ed.). Austin, TX: PRO-ED.

Schopler, E., Reichler, R., & Renner, B. (1988). *Childhood Autism Rating Scale*. Los Angeles, CA: Western Psychological Services.

Schopler, E., Van Bourgondien, M. E., Wellman, G. J., & Love, S. R. (2010). *Childhood Autism Rating Scale* (2nd ed.). Los Angeles, CA: Western Psychological Services.

Semel, E., Wiig, E. H., & Secord, W. (2004). *Clinical Evaluation of Language Fundamentals–Preschool* (2nd ed.). San Antonio, TX: Harcourt Assessment.

Shea, V., & Mesibov, G. B. (2009). Age-related issues in the assessment of autism spectrum disorders. In S. Goldstein, J. A. Naglieri, & S. Ozonoff (Eds.), *Assessment of autism spectrum disorders* (pp. 117–137). New York, NY: Guilford Press.

Sparrow, S. S., Balla, D. A., & Cicchetti, D. V. (1984). *Vineland Adaptive Behavior Scales*. Circle Pines, MN: American Guidance Services.

Sparrow, S. S., Cicchetti, D. V., & Balla, D. A. (2005). *Vineland Adaptive Behavior Scales* (2nd ed.). Circle Pines, MN: American Guidance Services.

United States Government Accountability Office. (2005). *Special education: Children with autism*. Retrieved from http://gao.gov/new.items/d05220.pdf

Wechsler, D. (2001). *Wechsler Individual Achievement Test* (2nd ed.). San Antonio, TX: Harcourt Assessment.

Wechsler, D. (2002). *Wechsler Preschool and Primary Scale of Intelligence* (3rd ed.). San Antonio, TX: Psychological Corporation.

Wechsler, D. (2003). *Wechsler Intelligence Scale for Children* (4th ed.). San Antonio, TX: Psychological Corporation.

Wiig, E. H., & Secord, W. (1989). *Test of Language Competence*. New York, NY: Psychological Corporation.

Wing, L., & Potter, D. (2009). The epidemiology of autism spectrum disorders. Is the prevalence rising? In S. Goldstein, J. A. Naglieri, & S. Ozonoff (Eds.), *Assessment of autism spectrum disorders* (pp. 18–54). New York, NY: Guilford Press.

Woodcock, R. W., McGrew, K. S., & Mather, N. (2001). *Woodcock-Johnson III Tests of Cognitive Abilities*. Itasca, IL: Riverside.

Zimmerman, I., Steiner, V., & Pond, R. (2002). *Preschool Language Scale* (4th ed.). San Antonio, TX: Psychological Corporation.

chapter 3

Strategies for Teaching Kids With Autism

Christine Hoffner Barthold

Tell me and I'll forget; show me and I may
remember; involve me and I'll understand.

Chinese Proverb

THIS chapter will cover some general strategies for teaching students with ASD. Many of these strategies should be applicable to any student in any classroom, with some adaptations and creativity. Not too long ago, many students with ASD were considered unteachable and were placed in institutions or substandard settings (Scott, Clark, & Brady, 2000). Presently there is a shift toward more inclusive settings where students with ASD are educated alongside their typically developing peers. It can be difficult to choose what strategies will work best for students with ASD, particularly because there is not one strategy that has proven to be most effective for all students with ASD (National Research Council, 2001). In addition, many teachers and other professionals have had little autism-specific coursework to prepare them (Schwartz & Drager, 2008). A list of quick tips and tricks, although appealing, does not adequately address the needs of individuals with ASD or answer pressing questions about the best interventions to choose from the myriad available today. Therefore, having a good foundation of general instructional practices and an understanding of how to weigh the evidence is crucial. This is also important for parents. The financial investment in interventions can be significant; therefore, choosing those based in solid science is more cost-effective than those that may not have a scientific foundation. When evaluating educational programs for their child, it is important that parents look to see whether the research-based strategies described in this chapter and elsewhere in this book are being used. Otherwise, families and schools may be wasting time and money.

Choosing Strategies

Choosing effective strategies from the many that exist can be a challenge for parents and teachers alike. A recent study identified more than 100 different types of strategies often used by parents and clinicians, from behavioral therapy to biological interventions (Green et al., 2006). Parents often try multiple strategies in the hope that one will make a difference. Unfortunately, for many of these strategies, there just is not enough evidence to support that they work. Even when common sense prevails, our common sense can be wrong. It is thus very important that recommended strategies are "evidence based." This fact was highlighted in the No Child Left Behind Act (NCLB, 2001), which incorporated a number of standard-based principles of education reform. One of the standards in NCLB emphasizes an increase in quality of education by incorporating the use of scientifically based instructional strategies.

What does it mean to use evidence-based strategies? Many experts (e.g., Dunst, Trivette, & Cutspec, 2002; Odom, Collet-Klingenberg,

Rogers, & Hatton, 2010; Reichow, Doehring, Cicchetti, & Volkmar, 2011) have attempted to define evidence-based strategies. All agree that the core part of the definition is that there must be clear and unambiguous evidence that the use of a strategy resulted in improvements in student responding. The effectiveness must be demonstrated within the context of research studies that are designed so that other possible explanations can be ruled out. Accessing information on which strategies are considered to be evidence based has been made easier by the publication of several articles (available online) that review evidence-based strategies with respect to teaching students with ASD (e.g., National Autism Center, 2008; Odom, Collet-Klingenberg, et al., 2010).

It is somewhat beyond the scope of this chapter to provide an in-depth analysis of all of the different evidence-based strategies available for students with ASD. However, what follows is a brief overview of some of the more frequently used evidence-based strategies for ASD as well as a few that are popular, but not necessarily evidence based. Interventions and treatment models are broken down into the following categories: (1) evidence-based interventions, which consist of specific strategies that can be incorporated into any curriculum and/or setting (Odom, Collet-Klingenberg, et al., 2010); (2) evidence-based comprehensive treatment models (CTMs; Odom, Boyd, Hall, & Hume, 2010), which are usually multicomponent treatment packages systematically designed to be implemented over extended periods of time and to address core symptoms of ASD; (3) CTMs that are not evidence based but that rely upon evidence-based strategies; and (4) popular strategies and CTMs that do not have an empirical evidence base at this time. Finally, we will end this chapter discussing the evidence-based strategy of Positive Behavior Supports (PBS) and some critical strategies for understanding and replacing challenging behaviors.

Evidence-Based Strategies

Many of the evidence-based strategies used with students with ASD are based on the principles of applied behavior analysis (ABA).

In ABA, there is an emphasis on breaking complex skills into observable, measurable components. These components are taught with clear instructions and specific reinforcement for appropriate responding. Many students with ASD do best when both instructions and feedback are clear and concrete. ABA provides a system for doing so and helps students learn appropriate skills quickly and efficiently. Interventions are often based upon the strengths and needs of the child. An emphasis upon what triggers responding (i.e., antecedents) and what motivates or reduces responding (i.e., consequences) is emphasized (Bailey & Burch, 2006).

A recent comprehensive review of the literature revealed 24 evidence-based practices for use with students with ASD, with the majority of these practices using some sort of ABA (Odom, Collet-Klingenberg, et al., 2010). Eight of the 24 more commonly-used strategies described will be discussed: (1) reinforcement, (2) Discrete Trial Teaching, (3) naturalistic teaching strategies, (4) Picture Exchange Communication System (PECS), (5) teaching social skills, (6) prompting, (7) visual supports, and (8) structured work systems. The National Professional Development Center on Autism Spectrum Disorders' website (http://autismpdc.fpg.unc.edu) contains training modules, practice briefs, and implementation guidelines for more information regarding these and additional evidence-based strategies. It is important that teachers and parents obtain guidance and/or further training from a qualified professional when considering the use of the procedures described below.

Reinforcement

One of the most critical components of any teaching program for students with ASD is the systematic presentation of reinforcement for socially appropriate behavior. Whether or not materials are reinforcing is determined by their effect on behavior. In other words, materials are reinforcing if student behavior increases after the material is provided; if behavior does not increase, the material is not reinforcing regardless of how much a teacher thinks the material should be reinforcing or how reinforcing it is to other students in a classroom. It is also arguably the most important strategy; without it, other interventions will be far less potent.

The range of materials that may be reinforcing to a student is, in many respects, unlimited, depending on whether student behavior increases. Teachers will often use tangible materials (e.g., certificates, stickers, small toys, books, magazines, video games), privileges (e.g., team captain, line leader, passing out materials, sitting next to the teacher at lunch), or access to special activities (e.g., computer, DVD player, radio). The use of any of these should always be paired with social praise so that there is an increased likelihood that social praise will also become reinforcing. The most important point to remember is that everyone is different and so what is reinforcing to each student in a classroom may vary tremendously. That is why teachers and parents must select reinforcers from the perspective of the child, not what the adults might want the child to work for.

Concerns about students becoming dependent on concrete reinforcers are common. The fact is that all human beings are, to some extent, dependent upon concrete reinforcers. A person may love his job, but if he stopped getting paid for his work, it's doubtful that he would come to work indefinitely just for intrinsic motivation. The difference is that most adults with typical development have built up a tolerance to delay of reinforcement and can work for longer and longer periods of time without needing some sort of concrete reinforcer. This can also be true for students with ASD—at first, more concrete and contingent reinforcement might be necessary, but with careful planning students can gradually build up their tolerance so that more delayed and natural reinforcers (i.e., the ones that typically motivate other students) can be utilized (Alberto & Troutman, 2009).

How are reinforcers identified? There are many formal assessments that can be used to assess reinforcement (e.g., Mason & Egel, 1995), but the simplest way to figure out what might be reinforcing is to place a child in an environment where she has many options and see what she gravitates toward. Typically, the things that students tend to pick when left to their own devices function well as reinforcers. Similar information can also be obtained by asking parents and previous teachers what materials have been used as reinforcers previously.

What about the student who doesn't seem to be motivated by anything? First of all, it is important to ensure that there are enough interesting choices available. Using the same reinforcer over and over again will often result in a decrease of responding, an indication that the reinforcer is no longer effective. Even for students who are motivated by praise, using the same phrase like "good job" can lose its effectiveness after a while. Teachers can decrease the likelihood of this happening by ensuring that they have a variety of preferred materials and activities available and by letting students choose what they want to work for during each teaching session. Teachers can also increase the novelty of materials by making some student preferences unavailable and then reintroducing them at a later time.

Identifying reinforcers is only the first step, however. It is important that items are used correctly to maximize their reinforcing potential. Parents and teachers should make sure that reinforcement is provided when children respond appropriately when the correct cue is provided. For example, it is more important to reinforce a student for tying his shoe when he sees that it is untied than in response to a teacher or parent saying, "Tie your shoe."

Reinforcement must also be provided immediately following the appropriate response, especially when students are just beginning to learn a skill. Waiting until the student comes home or it's convenient to provide a reinforcer will just confuse the student. It is also important for teachers to change the schedule of reinforcement once a student begins to learn the skill being taught. For example, as a student begins to learn a skill, a teacher might begin to provide reinforcement after the third or fourth correct response instead of reinforcing a student each time he responds correctly. Changing the schedule of reinforcement so that it is more intermittent is necessary in order to maintain the skill over time (Alberto & Troutman, 2009).

Keeping the teaching environment interesting and motivating, with related and natural reinforcers, will help students learn more

Table 3.1

Using Reinforcement

Tips	Example
• Be creative! Don't discount a reinforcer because it seems strange. Some individuals with autism are motivated by odd things like pieces of string. • Be sure to reinforce immediately after the required response, especially when a student is beginning to learn skills. Reinforcement should be reduced once a child begins to learn a skill so that it is provided only after some occurrences of the behavior (e.g., after every third response). • No freebies! If you decide to use something as a reinforcer, make sure the child earns it every time it's given to him. • Have a variety of ways that you reinforce the child's behavior—praise, tangible items (e.g., certificates, stickers, posters), privileges (e.g., team captain, line leader, choosing a TV program, choosing a snack) and/or activities (e.g., computer time, games, playing outside, special projects). • Always provide social praise when using other forms of reinforcement.	Janice, a parent of a 3-year-old with autism, knew that her child liked to drink juice and she wanted him to request juice when he was thirsty. At breakfast the next day, Janice gave her son an empty cup. When he said "juice," she immediately gave him a small amount of juice. When he drank it, he said "juice" again, and Janice was ready to give him more. He said "juice" about 20 times in a 15-minute period.

readily. For example, there is not really a motivation for a student with ASD to put on a coat unless she is going someplace cold; therefore, recess might be the ideal time for teaching that skill as opposed to "drill time." Similarly, individuals rarely ask for food unless they are hungry. Therefore, snack times and lunch might be a great time to practice requesting skills. Tips for using reinforcement and an example describing implementation can be found in Table 3.1.

Discrete Trial Teaching

Discrete Trial Teaching, or DTT, is probably one of the oldest and most effective strategies used for presenting instruction to students with ASD (e.g., Cohen, Amerine-Dickens, & Smith, 2006; Smith, 2001). (DTT is also known as Discrete Trial Instruction or DTI.) In a discrete trial, skills are broken down into very specific component parts and taught step by step. Smith (2001) identified five parts that form a discrete trial: (1) the discriminative stimulus or instruction, (2) teacher assistance (i.e., prompt) immediately before or after the instruction to help ensure a correct response, (3) the student response, (4) systematic reinforcement for correct responses or error correction, and (5) a short pause between trials.

The discriminative stimulus will vary among trials, but usually consists of some sort of short instruction (e.g., "touch your nose," "read the story," "get ready to go to lunch"). These instructions can either be very simple for students who are early learners or more complex as students acquire more skills. The student is expected to respond relatively quickly; although wait time between the discriminative stimulus and response varies among practitioners with accepted wait time typically between 2 and 5 seconds (Lovaas, 2002). It is also important that all individuals working with a student with ASD expect the same response. If one person accepts crouching as sitting down and another accepts only "criss-cross applesauce," the instruction and progression through the protocols can be rather inconsistent. The teacher, especially in the beginning of instruction, may prompt a correct response from the student in order to minimize errors. For example, the teacher may use hand-over-hand guidance to help the student be successful. The prompt is subsequently faded as the student learns the skill so that she ultimately learns to respond to the instruction alone.

A correct response should be followed with praise, preferred items, and/or a small amount of food, depending on what has been identified as reinforcing to the student. If the student responds incorrectly or fails to respond at all, some form of feedback is given to indicate to the student that her response was incorrect (e.g., "Let's try again) and the instruction is presented again, typically with teacher assistance. A short pause of 1–2 seconds separates the trials, which makes them

Table 3.2

Implementing Discrete Trial Teaching

Tips	Example
• Provide a brief, clear instruction or question that is appropriate to the skill being taught.	Tom, the teacher of Lisa, a 9-year-old with autism, is trying to teach coin identification and value using DTT.
• Reinforce the student if his response is correct and occurs within 5 seconds following the instruction.	*Tom*: "Lisa, give me the nickel and tell me how much it is worth"
• Deliver feedback for incorrect responses ("try again") and provide assistance (prompts) following the next instruction.	*Lisa: Hands teacher the nickel.* "This is a nickel, and it is worth five cents" *Tom*: "That's right! Good for you." *Pauses 1–5 seconds and presents next instruction.*
• Pause 1–5 seconds (intertrial interval) before presenting the instruction that starts the next trial. This helps to ensure that the student learns when one trial is completed and a new trial begins.	
• Before trying discrete trial teaching, consult a qualified behavior analyst for help. Many are listed at http://www.bacb.com.	

discrete (Smith, 2001). Table 3.2 provides tips for using DTT and an example describing implementation.

As mentioned previously, there is an enormous amount of evidence supporting the effectiveness of DTT. However, two limitations in particular have been identified. First, students may only learn to respond correctly when the teacher gives the instructions and not when the specific instruction is absent. For example, a student with ASD may learn to play with peers when the teacher says, "Go play with your friends"; however, he may not play with his friends if only the friends are present (natural cue for playing). A second concern is that students may have difficulty using the skills in settings outside of the classroom due to the highly structured nature of DTT (Naoi, 2009; Smith, 2001).

Naturalistic Teaching Strategies

Teachers and parents may be able to reduce problems with DTT by using naturalistic teaching strategies. These are strategies where the teacher follows the student's lead and/or contrives situations where communication and socialization can be facilitated. The reinforcers are considered to be more contextually relevant. For example, a favorite cookie might be placed in a clear container that the student is unable to open. Therefore, the student must ask an adult for assistance in accessing the cookie (the reinforcer). The key aspects of naturalistic strategies are the emphasis on the student's motivation and the usability of such strategies in everyday, naturally occurring events, such as in play, meal time, or completing homework. Strategies that utilize naturalistic teaching strategies include, but are not limited to, Pivotal Response Training (PRT; Koegel & Koegel, 2006) and Incidental Teaching (IT; c.f., McGee, Krantz, Mason, & McClannahan, 1983). Some people erroneously think that naturalistic strategies are different from ABA, when in fact they are a different application of the behavioral model. Reinforcement and error correction is systematic and based upon the student's response.

In naturalistic interventions, the teaching stimuli are chosen by the student; that is, things that the student is already interested in are used as the teaching stimuli. For example, if a student is picking up and spinning the wheels of a toy car, the teacher will use that car to teach a skill in the moment as opposed to taking away the car to be used later. The teacher will then create some opportunity for social interaction around this interesting and potentially reinforcing item. For example, the teacher might pick up the car and hold it expectantly while waiting for the student to ask (e.g., verbalize, sign, point to, give a picture) to play with the car. Once the student makes a close approximation of the response (e.g., "play car," "can I have car?"), the teacher will provide some sort of naturalistic reinforcement such as rolling the car back to the student. Because skills are taught in the natural environment using stimuli that the student already gravitates toward, there is a good probability that the student will apply the social and communication skills learned to the areas where they are most expected (Koegel & Koegel, 2006).

Table 3.3
Implementing Naturalistic Teaching

Tips	Example
• Use naturally occurring routines to teach. For example, have the child request food during meal time or identify items of clothing during dressing. • Do something unexpected, leave something out of a routine, or complete a task differently in order to entice the child to communicate. For example, during a mealtime, you might give a spoon but no food. When dressing, you might try to put the child's pants on her arms instead of her feet. • Arrange the environment so that children are more likely to initiate communication. For example, having a highly desirable item visible but out of reach is a good way to facilitate child-initiated requests. • If the child makes an attempt to communicate, reinforce it! Don't expect "please," "thank you," or complete sentences from the very beginning. • Keep teaching light and fun. If you feel like you're forcing too much, back off and try again later.	Hannah was teaching her 10-year-old daughter, Annalisa, to identify common self-care products. During bathtime, instead of handing Annalisa the shampoo, she handed her a toothbrush. When Annalisa looked confused, she picked up the shampoo and said, "shampoo." She then expected Annalisa to say the word "shampoo" back. At first, it sounded like "sha-sha," but Hannah was thrilled and gave Annalisa the shampoo.

Occasionally, the environment might be engineered or sabotaged in order to prompt the student to initiate communication. For example, a student might be given a worksheet but not a pencil. This situation would serve as a natural prompt to the student to subsequently ask for a pencil. Similarly, a teacher may place a student's favorite toys so that they are visible but out of reach. The student is more likely to initiate a request in this situation than if the toys were more readily accessible. Tips for using naturalistic teaching strategies are provided in Table 3.3, as well as an example showing their application.

Picture Exchange Communication System

It is essential that students with ASD be provided with and taught how to use functional communication systems immediately following diagnosis, given the profound communication problems that are so evident in these children. Nonverbal communication systems may be the most appropriate for the large number of students with ASD who have difficulty with verbal communication. The Picture Exchange Communication System (PECS; Bondy & Frost, 1994) is an evidenced-based communication system that methodically teaches students to communicate using picture symbols. Training takes place in six phases, where students are systematically taught more complex exchanges with a book of picture symbols. Putting pictures in a book and giving them to a student is not synonymous with PECS, nor is the act of having a student simply point to a picture included as part of the PECS procedure. The most important component of the PECS communication system is the exchange of the picture or object from one individual to another, which signals intentional communication between two people. In order for the system to be effective, it is important that these phases are taught as developed in the PECS manual. Furthermore, it is essential that the picture symbols are readily available to the student in *all* environments (including home and community; Frost & Bondy, 2002; Sulzer-Azaroff, Hoffman, Horton, Bondy, & Frost, 2009).

In a recent review of the literature, Ganz et al. (in press) found that PECS, along with other types of picture-based communication systems and voice output communication devices (often known as VOCA) improved communication skills in students with ASD. In addition to increasing communication, using an alternative form of communication also helped increase social skills and reduce problem behaviors. Therefore, providing alternative communication supports may lead to additional social and behavioral benefits (Ganz et al., in press).

Teaching Social Skills

Given that social relatedness is one of the defining features of ASD, several evidence-based strategies have been developed for teaching appropriate social behaviors. One area that has received considerable attention has been peer-mediated intervention (PMI). PMI includes strategies used to systematically teach typically peers and children with ASD how to engage in positive social interactions. Students as young as 3 have been used to help their peers with ASD increase social skills.

Peer-mediated interventions can be a beneficial part of the program for students with ASD, particularly if they are included with their typically developing peers. The implementation of such programs would require that classroom staff provide opportunities and training that would increase the likelihood of interactions between typical peers and students with ASD. Neitzel and colleagues (Neitzel, 2008; Sperry, Neitzel, & Engelhardt-Wells, 2010) noted that there were common steps present in many research studies on PMI. These included: (1) selecting peers who are well-liked and who interacted frequently with a variety of other students; (2) teaching peers how to engage students with ASD through teacher demonstration, role-play, and explicit reinforcement for using the skills correctly; (3) practice sessions with students with ASD during which staff provided suggestions to peers on how to initiate/maintain interactions; and (4) identifying/providing naturally occurring opportunities for interactions throughout the day so that social interactions will be more likely to generalize to other settings within the school. Tips for using peer modeling are presented in Table 3.4, as well as an example describing implementation.

Video modeling is another strategy that has been used to teach appropriate social behavior. The student watches a short video of competent individuals modeling appropriate social behavior. The advantage is that the student with ASD can watch the same video over and over, pause, and rewind, allowing for a level of practice not available with live models. Video modeling has been effective with students with autism (e.g., Delano, 2007) and has been identified as an evidence-based strategy (Odom, Collet-Klingenberg, et al., 2010).

With video modeling, the teacher defines a social behavior in observable and measurable terms (e.g., greeting strangers by saying "hello"). Teachers will then write a short, concrete script that breaks

Table 3.4

Using Peer Modeling

Tips	Example
• Children as young as 3 can be taught to be peer models. • Consider children that may not be "superstars" to be peer models. Children who are socially competent, interested in helping others, flexible, and cooperative often make excellent peer models. • Be sure that children with autism have plenty of opportunities to be with typical peers. • Give peer models specific instructions (e.g., tap your friend on the shoulder to get her attention, provide assistance by showing how to complete an activity) and facilitated practice on how to interact with a child with autism; don't just put them together and hope things goes well.	Sam, a child with autism, is included in a typical preschool. Ms. Boyle creates the "social butterflies" group and creates wings for all of its members. During group meetings, the children learn about topics such as initiating social interaction, sharing, and providing compliments. During the first 5 minutes of the group meeting, the children talk about the importance of each skill. Ms. Boyle models concrete ways to implement the social skill, like saying "Thank you" to someone who gives them a toy. Afterward, the group practices using role-playing. Ms. Boyle also points out how some of their friends may need to be reminded more than others about how to share and play together. During playtime, Ms. Boyle walks around and provides praise to the children using the skill she taught them during group time.

down the skill into its component parts (also known as a task analysis). Once the video is made, editing is often necessary to make sure that the necessary skills are modeled appropriately. Students view the video on their own schedule with or without adult assistance. Video modeling has been used successfully to teach a variety of social, play, and vocational skills to students with ASD (Allen, Wallace, & Renes, 2010). Tips for using video modeling and an example showing how it is done are presented in Table 3.5.

Prompting

The idea behind prompting is to provide additional support to a

Table 3.5
Using Video Modeling

Tips	Example
• Video models are available online, but videos shot with people familiar to the child or from the child's perspective often work best. • Keep the videos short and interesting. • Videos should show the child with autism exactly what to do in the new situation. • Review the video several times before the child is expected to enter the new situation. • Provide reinforcement when the skills are used in the natural environment.	Mary, a 16-year-old with autism, had been asked to leave several work placements due to meltdowns. Usually, these meltdowns happened during the first day of work or when an adult changed the tasks that were part of Mary's typical routine. Her teacher decided to make a video of her next job site placement from her perspective that starred her new colleagues and showed the tasks she was going to have to complete. Mary reviewed the video about 3–4 times before she went to her new job site, often rewinding and rewatching her favorite parts. The supervisors at the job site reported that Mary had very few problems her first day on the job.

student in order to ensure that he responds successfully. The more times a student is successful, the more reinforcement can be delivered, which increases the chances that the student will be successful in the future. There are many different ways to prompt a behavior. An example of a prompting sequence is *least-to-most prompting*. In least-to-most prompting, the teacher increases the level of assistance until the student is successful. For example, the teacher may point to the item that the student needs to complete an action. If the student does not respond, the teacher may model the response. If the student is still not successful, then the teacher may provide hand-over-hand assistance (Alberto & Troutman, 2009). More detailed reviews of other prompting systems can be found in Alberto and Troutman (2009) or Boutot and Smith Myles (2011). One of the most important aspects of prompting that teachers and parents need to remember is that prompts must eventually be faded (i.e., the use of the prompt is gradually reduced over time until the student can complete the task independently); otherwise students may learn to respond only when the prompt is used (Heflin & Alaimo, 2007).

Visual Supports

Many students with ASD are considered to be visual learners; that is, they acquire knowledge best when information is concrete and can be referenced easily. Visual supports, such as schedules, can help a student navigate the world around her by providing structure and predictability. Many people with ASD are literal and concrete interpreters of information. That is, they will most likely do exactly what they are told to do. Things like visual schedules can maximize students' success in independently following the routine and self-regulation surrounding transitions.

Picture schedules that function much like a to-do list are often very helpful for students on the autism spectrum (Banda, Grimmett, & Hart, 2009). Having clear signals that consistently are associated with transitions from one activity to another can really help a student become comfortable and more ready to learn. Teaching students what to do and *when* is critical to success (Hume, Loftin, & Lantz, 2009).

When creating a visual schedule, it is very important to tailor the schedule to the developmental level of the student. Younger children and students with lower cognitive skills will have trouble processing a schedule that includes all of the day's events. For these students, it might be helpful to begin with only what is happening now and what happens next. For others, a schedule that depicts a finite amount of time (e.g., the morning) may be more effective. Schedules typically move from left to right or top to bottom. A daily schedule for a student with ASD is shown in Figure 3.1. This example is for a written schedule, but pictures could also be used to represent the classes if the student could not read a written schedule.

With any type of visual system (e.g., communication device, work system, visual schedule), the ability of the student to process symbols must be considered. Although commercially available symbol systems are popular, they may be too abstract for early learners. Photos and/or

Period/Time	Class	Room #
1: 7:25–8:15	Math	223
2: 8:20–9:10	English	110
3: 9:15–10:05	Computer Lab	115
4: 10:10–11:00	P.E.	Gym
5: 11:10–11:30	Lunch	Cafeteria
6: 11:40–1:40	Community/Work	
7: 1:50–2:20	Social Group	122
8: 2:30–Dismissal		

Figure 3.1. Daily schedule for a high school student with ASD.

actual items might be more appropriate for these students. For more advanced students, a written to-do list may be sufficient—remember that letters are symbols, too. It is important that when visuals are created that the developmental level of the child, the complexity of the task, and the legibility of the symbols are all taken into account (Mineo Mollica, Virion, Gray, & Pennington, 2005).

Structured Work Systems

A goal for most students on the autism spectrum is independence. However, many times, instructional methodologies and interventions can foster dependence upon others for prompting and reinforcement (Heflin & Alaimo, 2007). Structured work systems were developed to help the student with ASD organize and sequence tasks in a concrete way. These systems often work in tandem with visual supports. According to Carnahan, Hume, Clarke, and Borders (2009), the work system should explicitly show the student what to do, how many items to complete, when the work is ended, and what to do once the work is done.

Especially for beginners, the system moves from left to right and items are arranged in sequence. For example, a teacher might be teaching a student how to sort utensils and bag them for a local eatery. The beginning of a work system might have a set of utensils and a set of zipper bags. The student matches the knife, fork, and spoon to a model and puts them in a bag. That bag is then put into another container to the right of the student. Once all of the bags are filled, the student can access the CD player at the end of the work system. Teaching is done through the least obtrusive prompting system necessary, using few verbal prompts to insure independence. Structured work systems can be used for vocational tasks or academic tasks—anything that has a sequence.

Evidence-Based Comprehensive Treatment Models (CTMs)

Two recent reviews of the literature (National Autism Center, 2008; Odom, Boyd, et al., 2010) gathered the evidence of available treatment studies of students with ASD. As with evidence-based strategies, the CTMs with the most supportive evidence are for the most part based upon ABA. The CTMs identified by Odom, Boyd, et al. (2010) as having the strongest evidence included LEAP (Hoyson, Jamieson, & Strain, 1984), the May Institute (Campbell et al., 1998), the Princeton Child Development Institute (Fenske, Zalenski, Krantz, & McClannahan, 1985), the Lovaas Institute (Cohen et al., 2006), and the Early Start Denver Model (Rogers & Dawson, 2010). Two of these CTMs are highlighted below. If you are interested in learning more about identified CTMs, we encourage you to read the National Autism Center's report and Odom, Boyd, et al. (2010).

Lovaas Institute

O. Ivar Lovaas was one of the first individuals to create a CTM for students with ASD. Building upon work by individuals such as Ferster (1961), Lovaas created a curriculum that included teaching expressive communication, receptive communication, imitation, matching and sorting, and social behaviors. These behaviors were primarily taught through Discrete Trial Teaching. Although typically implemented in the home, Lovaas programs are also implemented in schools and clinics. Intervention is intensive; 35–40 hours per week is considered to be optimal for success. At present, the Lovaas model has the most evidence for effectiveness, with at least three studies supporting that individuals make better gains with this model than other, more eclectic interventions (Howard, Sparkman, Cohen, Green, & Stanislaw, 2005).

Early Start Denver Model (ESDM)

This model is the most recent of all of the evidence-based models presented, but has a rich history. The Early Start Denver Model (Rogers & Dawson, 2010) is a model of early intervention that bases its techniques upon ABA, brain and neurological research, and cognitive science (i.e., research into how we think and process information). It is an interdisciplinary, parent training model. The intervention is based upon increasing social interactions with adults and focuses heavily on imitation, verbal and nonverbal communication, and play skills. Skills are taught so that they are fluent, reciprocal, flexible, and spontaneous. The intervention incorporates traditional ABA, the play-based elements of naturalistic teaching, and the Denver Model. In the Denver Model, adults modulate and model positive affect and provide positive interactions in a developmentally appropriate way. Parents must be extremely involved in this model, and intervention is intensive (ideally, happening throughout the day).

The ESDM has been validated by a randomized study. This type of study is considered to be the gold standard of science. In a randomized study, participants are randomly assigned to a treatment group (in this case, ESDM) or a control group (in this case, typical community-based interventions). Average performance of the groups was compared at the end of the first and second years to see if there is any difference between them. Children in the ESDM group made more progress than their peers in typical community-based interventions (Dawson et al., 2010).

Comprehensive Treatment Models That Incorporate Evidence-Based Strategies

There are CTMs that have not been tested empirically, but nonetheless incorporate evidence-based strategies such as discrete trials or structured work systems. Three examples of these CTMs are TEACCH, Applied Verbal Behavior, and Social Thinking.

TEACCH

TEACCH stands for Treatment and Education of Autistic and related Communication handicapped Children; however, it's best known by its acronym. Created in the early 1970s by Dr. Eric Schopler and his colleagues in North Carolina, TEACCH emphasizes altering the environment to capitalize upon the strengths of many students with ASD and to promote their independence. Interventions in TEACCH build upon what are considered to be strengths of a lot of kids with ASD: structured environments, visual cues and schedules, and emphasis on routines. Structured work systems and visual supports and schedules are critical components of TEACCH. Although TEACCH does not have as much evidence to support its use in schools, two small and well-designed studies support its effectiveness (Hume & Odom, 2007; Ozonoff & Cathcart, 1998). Therefore, while more research needs to be done with regard to TEACCH, it is a treatment model that provides systematic and visually based instruction that teachers and parents might consider for their students with ASD.

Applied Verbal Behavior

Applied Verbal Behavior (AVB) combines the more strict drill-based structure of DTT and the more naturalistic characteristics of PRT/IT to teach students to communicate and socialize. The main focus of AVB is the function of language, something that Skinner (1957) called "verbal operants." In general, AVB focuses on the following verbal operants: manding, which is any type of request or protest;

tacting, which is labeling items; receptive language; imitation; and intraverbals, which is the use of language for social means (akin to casual conversation). Self-help skills such as feeding and dressing are also addressed. Unlike traditional DTT, skills are mixed within teaching sessions and mand (request) training is a main focus, especially for beginning learners.

Social Thinking

A relatively new strategy popular for students with mild autism and Asperger's syndrome is Social Thinking, developed by Michelle Garcia-Winner. In Social Thinking, there is more of an emphasis on the cognitive-behavioral aspects of social skills; specifically, taking the perspective of others. In Social Thinking, students learn why social skills are important and how these skills translate into better relationships with others. Social skills, such as learning to be with a group, self-awareness, keeping comments and questions quiet until a good opportunity presents itself, and using one's imagination, are taught via structured activity, analysis of videotapes, self-monitoring, books, and visual aids (Garcia-Winner, 2008). Although Garcia-Winner stated that the exercises in her manual are based upon the science of cognitive behavior therapy, to date there is only one small research study that supports its effectiveness (Crooke, Hendrix, & Rachman, 2008). Therefore, while Social Thinking may be a promising strategy for individuals with more mild ASDs, more research needs to be done before it can be considered to be an evidence-based practice.

Popular Strategies, but Not Evidence Based

There are many strategies and CTMs for students with ASD that are popular, but lack empirical evidence to support them. These include sensory-based strategies, DIR/Floortime, biomedical and dietary interventions, and Relationship Development Intervention

(RDI). As with previous sections, it is not possible to list all of the popular non-evidence-based treatments. The purpose of this section is to familiarize the reader with treatments that are commonly encountered in a school setting.

Sensory-Based Strategies

Several authors have noted that individuals with ASD exhibit behaviors that suggest the presence of sensory dysfunction. Schaaf (2011) noted that such a dysfunction may impact a person's ability to engage in a variety of behaviors (e.g., play, social behaviors, self-care skills). Within school programs, occupational therapists typically design and implement, with the help of classroom staff, strategies for responding to sensory dysfunction. The activities chosen are based on the individual's needs as identified through a comprehensive assessment. For example, staff may increase a student's vestibular experiences through swinging or other forms of movement, use joint compression or weighted vests in order to provide "deep pressure" to specific points on the body, or might brush the student's arms and legs with a dry brush. The assumption is that these types of activities will help address the sensory needs of students with ASD so that processing of sensory information is more efficient (Devlin, Leader, & Healy, 2009).

Unfortunately, there is little research that supports the effectiveness of such strategies. Studies that have suggested that sensory strategies are effective have not been completed in a manner that supports such conclusions. The lack of evidence has led investigators to conclude that, at the present time, there is not enough evidence to include sensory stimulation techniques as an evidence-based strategy (e.g., Schaaf, 2011; Thompson, 2007).

DIR/Floortime

Floortime, or the Developmental, Individual Differences, Relationship-Based (DIR) model was developed by Drs. Stanley Greenspan and Serena Wieder. This model focuses on engagement with adults and nonverbal behaviors. In Floortime, the therapist follows the student's lead, using the student's natural preferences and interaction style to build interactions. The purpose of Floortime is to develop social-affective, communication, and cognitive skills within a healthy emotional environment (Greenspan & Wieder, 2006). Even though Floortime has been used for more than 20 years, there is surprisingly little evidence to support its effectiveness. Only one small study is available that supports the use of Floortime (Solomon, Nechles, Ferch, & Bruckman, 2007). Much more research into Floortime needs to be done.

Restricted Diets and Biomedical Interventions

Hyman and Levy (2011) noted that many families include dietary restrictions as part of the overall interventions applied to their children with ASD. Teachers, of course, would not be responsible for implementing any type of dietary or medical interventions on their own. They might, however, be asked by parents to restrict certain foods in an attempt to control the symptoms of autism in the students they serve. For example, many families have their children with ASD on a diet that limits intakes of gluten (found in grain products) and casein (found in dairy products) because gluten-free and casein-free (GFCF) diets have been reported to reduce behaviors characteristic of individuals with ASD. Unfortunately, there is not enough evidence to support the use of GFCF diets with individuals with ASD. In a recent review of the studies on GFCF diets, Mulloy, Lang, O'Reilly, Sigafoos, and Lancioni (2010) found that current research does not support the effectiveness of GFCF diets with individuals with ASD.

Relationship Development Intervention (RDI)

Developed by Dr. Steven Gutstein, RDI is designed to teach students how to share experiences on a social level, which is often impaired in students with ASD. Parents are the main interventionists in RDI, with assistance from a trained and certified RDI consultant. Activities typically involve some sort of give-and-take play, starting with simple activities (such as banging on a drum) to more elaborate imaginative play (such as dress-up). On the RDI website, the developers claim that such activities, when done in a developmentally appropriate sequence, increase neural connections, allow students to be more flexible in their thinking, and increase social interactions (see http://www.rdiconnect. com/pages/our-programs.aspx for more information). At present, there is one small study done by Dr. Gutstein and his colleagues supporting its effectiveness (Gutstein, Burgess, & Montfort, 2007). Although some parents report success with RDI, much more research is needed before it can be considered an evidence-based strategy.

The Importance of Teaching for Application

No matter what type of strategy is chosen, teachers and parents must consider how they will ensure that students apply what they learned to the right environments. Just because a student can do a skill during drills at a table or choose the correct response during a role-play *does not* mean that she will be able to do this anywhere else. For most kids, it is sufficient for them to learn something in one or two environments. Their behavior then *generalizes* to novel situations, items, or people. That is, they are able to apply what they learned. Unfortunately, this is not so for many students with ASD. Therefore, it is important to teach in as many environments as possible, and make sure that students maintain what they have learned over time (Albin & Horner, 1988).

In order to ensure that what we teach generalizes to new environments, it is also important to introduce novel people and stimuli and require more than just rote responses from students. It is true that it takes a community to teach students with autism. "Teachers" of students with autism may include family members, individuals in the community, friends, and peers.

Handling Problem Behavior Through Positive Behavior Support

Many students with ASD have problem behaviors such as meltdowns, aggression, or strict adherence to routines. Often, the first response by parents or teachers might be to punish the behavior and make sure that it never happens again. However, that can backfire. Evidence suggests that Positive Behavior Supports (PBS) is the most effective strategy for handling problem behavior presented by students with ASD. In PBS, the reasons behind problem behavior are assessed through a process called Functional Behavioral Assessment (FBA). A more socially acceptable alternative is then taught to the student and systematically reinforced.

The fact is that if a student is repeatedly engaging in problem behavior, that behavior is probably being reinforced in some way. There are considered to be four main reinforcers for problem behavior, sometimes called functions: attention, escape, access to items, and automatic reinforcement (something internal that's not easily measured; Floyd, Phaneuf, & Wilczynski, 2005). Typically, however, outside forces are reinforcing problem behavior; for example, the well-meaning cashier who gives the student a lollipop in line in order to stop him from crying or a parent rushing to comfort a student who is having a severe meltdown. These seem like they are reasonable responses. Doing any of the above will stop the problem behavior for the time being, but for the student with ASD, these acts might serve to increase that problem behavior in the future.

Just because something seems to be reinforcing or punishing to a person doesn't mean that it will be so. For some students, attention of any kind—yelling, praise, being singled out—can be reinforcing. For other students, time-out can be quite reinforcing, because they are escaping a situation they don't want to be in anyway. It is not uncommon to see teachers and parents attempt to talk to a student while they are engaging in problem behavior, hoping to explain to them what they are doing wrong. For students with typical development, this may be an effective means of decreasing problem behavior. Most students with ASD do not have the communication skills to process what the teacher is telling them or the immediate self-regulation skills to change the behavior once they are upset. More importantly, the student has now initiated a social interaction with problem behavior.

The first part of addressing problem behavior is to figure out the function. Typically, that is done through observation. What are the things that are happening before the problem behavior occurs, and what are the things that are happening after the problem behavior occurs? What might be triggering or reinforcing the problem behavior? This process is known as Functional Behavioral Assessment (FBA). Teachers may be familiar with the FBA process; when done correctly, the research supports that it is an effective tool for decreasing problem behavior. Parents should request an FBA if they think there are any behavior problems that might impede learning. Tips for conducting an FBA, along with an example, are presented in Table 3.6.

Once the reinforcer for problem behavior is identified, care should be taken to eliminate or reduce the amount of reinforcement the student receives for problem behavior. *Extinction* is the contingent removal of consequences for previously reinforced behavior. For example, a student has a tantrum to receive a candy bar in the grocery store. In the past, her mother has given in, but this time she puts her foot down.

Extinction is a very powerful tool for decreasing behavior, but there are some caveats to its use. Things often get worse before they get better. This is called an *extinction burst*. If a caregiver gives in and reinforces behavior when it's at its worst, there is a risk of problem behavior becoming consistently worse. However, if the caregivers are consistent with extinction, problem behavior will soon decrease dramatically.

The other thing to keep in mind when using extinction is the concept of *differential reinforcement*. If extinction is used exclusively, the student has no idea what he is supposed to do instead. So, he'll come up with something to replace the behavior—most likely another problem behavior. For example, it is determined that a student hits to get out of

Table 3.6

Conducting Functional Behavioral Assessment

Tips	Example
• An FBA is required in school whenever a problem behavior impedes a child's learning. • An FBA at a minimum should include: information about the classroom from teachers as well as instructional assistants, direct observation data about what parts of the environment might trigger problem behavior, and a statement about the possible function of the problem behavior. • It's rare that behavior serves a sensory function; usually, behavior serves to get something (positive reinforcement) or get out of/put off something unpleasant (negative reinforcement). Try to rule out triggers in the environment first before deciding that the behavior is internal. • Parents who want to get an idea of why a child is doing what she does can write down what happened immediately before the behavior occurred and what happened immediately after (see the example in this table). Look for patterns to emerge after several days that will help identify possible functions of the behavior • For severe behavior problems (e.g., self-injury, severe aggression), seek the help of a qualified behavior analyst.	Sal, a 5-year-old with autism, would often start to complain loudly around dinnertime. Sal's father, Jack, decided to keep a journal where he wrote down what happened right before Sal began complaining and what happened immediately after he complained. What Jack found was that Sal would often start complaining right as he started cooking dinner, and that it would often increase when he told Sal sternly to "be quiet." Jack hypothesized that Sal complained in order to get his attention. Armed with that knowledge, Jack started making sure that Sal was engaged with a puzzle or another activity before he started dinner. He checked on Sal frequently and praised him when he was quiet. If Sal started to whine, Jack ignored him. After a short time, Sal complained a lot less than he did before.

a difficult task (escape). Therefore, the team decides that it will no longer allow the student to escape the task contingent upon problem behavior. Hitting goes down, but after a while, the student starts biting in place of hitting and the process begins again. It might be better to teach the student to ask for a break when she feels overwhelmed. Over time, it is possible to decrease the number of breaks and have the student working at a steady pace. If a student didn't know how to read, add, or play, then the adults in her environment would teach her, not punish her for not knowing what to do. The same approach should be taken when addressing inappropriate behavior (Petscher & Bailey, 2008).

Conclusion

Teaching students with autism may seem different, but most of these ideas will sound very familiar. The most important things to remember are to (1) work as a team, (2) try different things, (3) refer to the research, and (4) plan individually for success. Each of these topics will be discussed throughout the various chapters in this book; however, it is important to remember that with those four critical elements, students with autism will have an important foundation for success.

References

Alberto, P. A., & Troutman, A. C. (2009). *Applied behavior analysis for teachers* (8th ed.). Upper Saddle River, NJ: Merrill-Prentice-Hall.

Albin, R. W., & Horner, R. H. (1988). Generalization with precision. In R. H. Horner, G. Dunlap, & R. L. Koegel (Eds.), *Generalization and maintenance: Life-style changes in applied settings* (pp. 99–120). Baltimore, MD: Brookes.

Allen, K. D., Wallace, D. P., & Renes, D. (2010). Use of video modeling to teach vocational skills to adolescents and young adults with autism spectrum disorders. *Education and Treatment of Children, 33,* 339–349.

Bailey, J. S., & Burch, M. (2006). *How to think like a behavior analyst.* New York, NY: Routledge.

Banda, D. R., Grimmett, E., & Hart, S. L. (2009). Helping students with autism spectrum disorders in general education classrooms manage transition issues. *Teaching Exceptional Children, 41,* 16–21.

Bondy, A. S., & Frost, L. A. (1994). The picture exchange communication system. *Focus on Autistic Behavior, 9*, 1–19.

Boutot, E. A., & Smith Myles, B. (2011). *Autism spectrum disorders: Foundations, characteristics, and effective strategies.* Upper Saddle River, NJ: Pearson.

Campbell, S., Cannon, B., Ellis, J. T., Lifter, K., Luiselli, J. K., Navalta, C. P., & Taras, M. (1998). The May Center for early childhood education: Description of a continuum of services model for children with autism. *International Journal of Disability, Development and Education, 45*, 173–187.

Carnahan, C. R., Hume, K., Clarke, L., & Borders, C. (2009). Using structured work systems to promote independence and engagement for students with autism spectrum disorders. *Teaching Exceptional Children, 41*, 6–14.

Cohen, H., Amerine-Dickens, M., & Smith, T. (2006). Early intensive behavioral treatment: Replication of the UCLA Model in a community setting. *Developmental and Behavioral Pediatrics, 27*, 145–155.

Crooke, P. J., Hendrix, R. E., & Rachman, J. Y. (2008). Brief report: Measuring the effectiveness of teaching social thinking to children with Asperger syndrome (AS) and high functioning autism (HFA). *Journal of Autism and Developmental Disorders, 38*, 581–591.

Dawson, G., Rogers, S., Munson, J., Smith, M., Winter, J., Greenson, J., & Varley, J. (2010). Randomized, controlled trial of an intervention for toddlers with autism: The Early Start Denver Model. *Pediatrics, 125*, e17–e23.

Delano, M. E. (2007). Video modeling interventions for individuals with autism. *Remedial and Special Education, 28*, 33–42.

Devlin, S., Leader, G., & Healy, O. (2009). Comparison of behavioral intervention and sensory-integration therapy in the treatment of self-injurious behavior. *Research in Autism Spectrum Disorders, 3*, 223–231.

Dunst, C. J., Trivette, C. M., & Cutspec, P. A. (2002). *Toward an operational definition of evidence-based practice.* Ashville, NC: Winterberry Press.

Fenske, E. C., Zalenski, S., Krantz, P. J., & McClannahan, L. E. (1985). Age at intervention and treatment outcome for autistic children in a comprehensive intervention program. *Analysis and Intervention in Developmental Disabilities, 5*, 49–58.

Ferster, C. F. (1961). Reinforcement and behavioral deficits of autistic children. *Child Development, 32*, 437–456.

Floyd, R. G., Phaneuf, R. L., & Wilczynski, S. M. (2005). Measurement properties of indirect assessment methods for functional behavioral assessment: A review of research. *School Psychology Review, 34*, 58–73.

Frost, L. A., & Bondy, A. S. (2002). *The picture exchange communication system training manual* (2nd ed.). Newark, DE: Pyramid Educational Consultants.

Ganz, J. B., Earles-Vollrath, T. L., Heath, A. K., Parker, R. I., Rispoli, M. J., & Duran, J. B. (in press). A meta-analysis of single case research studies on aided augmentative communication systems with individuals with autism spectrum disorders. *Journal of Autism and Developmental Disorders.*

Garcia-Winner, M. (2008). *Think social! A social thinking curriculum for school-age students*. San Jose, CA: Think Social.

Green, V. A., Pituch, K. A., Itchon, J., Choi, A., O'Reilly, M., & Sigafoos, J. (2006). Internet survey of treatments used by parents of children with autism. *Research in Developmental Disabilities, 27*, 70–84.

Greenspan, S. I., & Wieder, S. (2006). *Engaging autism*. Cambridge, MA: Da Capo Press.

Gutstein, S. E., Burgess, A. F., & Montfort, K. (2007). Evaluation of the relationship development intervention program. *Autism, 11*, 397–411.

Heflin, L. J., & Alaimo, D. F. (2007). *Students with autism spectrum disorders: Effective instructional practices*. Upper Saddle River, NJ: Pearson.

Howard, J. S., Sparkman, C. R., Cohen, H. G., Green, G., & Stanislaw, H. (2005). A comparison of intensive behavior analytic and eclectic treatments for young children with autism. *Research in Developmental Disabilities: A Multidisciplinary Journal, 26*, 359–383.

Hoyson, M., Jamieson, B., & Strain, P. S. (1984). Individualized group instruction of normally developing and autistic-like children: The LEAP curriculum model. *Journal of the Division of Early Childhood, 8*, 157–172.

Hume, K., Loftin, R., & Lantz, J. (2009). Increasing independence in autism spectrum disorders: A review of three focused interventions. *Journal of Autism and Developmental Disorders, 39,* 1329–1338.

Hume, K., & Odom, S. (2007). Effects of an individual work system on the independent functioning of students with autism. *Journal of Autism and Developmental Disorders, 37,* 1166–1180.

Hyman, S. L., & Levy, S. E. (2011). Dietary, complementary, and alternative therapies. In B. Reichow, P. Doehring, D. Cicchetti, & F. R. Volkmar (Eds.), *Evidence-based practices and treatments for children with autism* (pp. 275–293). New York, NY: Springer.

Koegel, R. L., & Koegel, L. K. (2006). *Pivotal response treatments for autism.* Baltimore, MD: Brookes.

Lovaas, O. I. (2002). *Teaching individuals with developmental delays: Basic intervention techniques.* Austin, TX: PRO-ED.

Mason, S. A., & Egel, A. L. (1995). What does Amy like? Using a mini-reinforcer assessment to increase student participation in instructional activities. *Teaching Exceptional Children, 28,* 42–45.

McGee, G. G., Krantz, P. J., Mason, D., & McClannahan, L. E. (1983). A modified incidental-teaching procedure for autistic youth: Acquisition and generalization of receptive object labels. *Journal of Applied Behavior Analysis, 16,* 329–338.

Mineo Mollica, B., Virion, C., Gray, J., & Pennington, C. (2005, November). *Customizing language representations to individual strengths and needs.* Presented at the annual convention of the American Speech-Language-Hearing Association Convention, San Diego, CA.

Mulloy, A., Lang, R., O'Reilly, M., Sigafoos, J., & Lancioni, G. (2010). Gluten-free and casein-free diets in the treatment of autism spectrum disorders: A systematic review. *Research in Autism Spectrum Disorders, 4,* 328–339.

Naoi, N. (2009). Interventions and treatment methods for children with autism spectrum disorders. In J. L. Matson (Ed.), *Applied behavior analysis for children with autism spectrum disorders* (pp. 67–81). New York, NY: Springer.

National Autism Center. (2008). *National standards project.* Retrieved from http://www.nationalautismcenter.org/about/national.php

National Research Council. (2001). *Educating children with autism.* Washington, DC: National Academy Press.

Neitzel, J. (2008). *Implementation checklist for PMI: Early childhood.* Chapel Hill: University of North Carolina, The National Professional Development Center on Autism Spectrum Disorders, Frank Porter Graham Child Development Institute.

No Child Left Behind Act, 20 U.S.C. §6301 (2001).

Odom, S., Boyd, B., Hall, L., & Hume, K. (2010). Evaluation of comprehensive treatment models for individuals with autism spectrum disorders. *Journal of Autism and Developmental Disorders, 40,* 425–436.

Odom, S. L., Collet-Klingenberg, L., Rogers, S. J., & Hatton, D. D. (2010). Evidence-based practices in interventions for children and youth with autism spectrum disorders. *Preventing School Failure, 54,* 275–282.

Ozonoff, S., & Cathcart, K. (1998). Effectiveness of a home program intervention for young children with autism. *Journal of Autism and Developmental Disorders, 28,* 25–32.

Petscher, E. S., & Bailey, J. S. (2008). Comparing main and collateral effects of extinction and differential reinforcement of alternative behavior. *Behavior Modification, 32,* 468–488.

Reichow, B., Doehring, P., Cicchetti, D. V., & Volkmar, F. R. (Eds.). (2011). *Evidence-based practices and treatments for children with autism.* New York, NY: Springer Science + Business Media.

Rogers, S., & Dawson, G. (2010). *Early Start Denver Model for young children with autism: Promoting language, learning, and engagement.* New York, NY: Guilford Press.

Schaaf, R. C. (2011). Interventions that address sensory dysfunction for individuals with autism spectrum disorders: Preliminary evidence for the superiority of sensory integration compared to other sensory approaches. In B. Reichow, P. Doehring, D. Cicchetti, & F. R. Volkmar (Eds.), *Evidence-based practices and treatments for children with autism* (pp. 245–273). New York, NY: Springer

Schwartz, H., & Drager, K. D. R. (2008). Training and knowledge in autism among speech-language pathologists: A survey. *Language, Speech, and Hearing Services in Schools, 39,* 66–77.

Scott, J., Clark, C., & Brady, M. P. (2000). *Students with autism: Characteristics and instructional programming for special educators*. San Diego, CA: Singular.

Skinner, B. F. (1957). *Verbal behavior*. Englewood Cliffs, NJ: Prentice Hall.

Smith, T. (2001). Discrete trial training in the treatment of autism. *Focus on Autism and Other Developmental Disabilities, 16*, 86–92.

Solomon, R., Nechles, J., Ferch, C., & Bruckman, D. (2007). Pilot study of a parent training program for young children with autism: The PLAY project home consultation program. *Autism, 11*, 205–224.

Sperry, L., Neitzel, J., & Engelhardt-Wells, K. (2010). Peer-mediated instruction and intervention strategies for students with autism spectrum disorders. *Preventing School Failure: Alternative Education for Children and Youth, 54*, 256–264.

Sulzer-Azaroff, B., Hoffman, A. O., Horton, C. B., Bondy, A., & Frost, L. (2009). The picture exchange communication system (PECS): What do the data say? *Focus on Autism and Other Developmental Disabilities, 24*, 89–103.

Thompson, T. (2007). *Making sense of autism*. Baltimore, MD: Brookes.

chapter 4

Educating the Preschool Student With Autism Spectrum Disorder

Katherine C. Holman

> The important thing is not so much that
> every child should be taught, as that every
> child should be given the wish to learn.
>
> John Lubbock

THE true essence of learning is unlocking the capacity and curiosity to seek more information and use this new knowledge to build on previous discoveries that encourage further inquiries. Teachers who recognize this purpose are those who understand how to make knowledge meaningful and relevant and to foster this cycle at an early age to inspire continued learning throughout one's lifetime. These facets of learning are the same for students with autism spectrum disorder (ASD); it just requires a deeper understanding of individual differences in learning and principles related to motivation.

Honoring and Respecting All Children and Individual Differences

Teachers most likely have had or will have the opportunity to have a student with ASD in their classrooms in recent years, given the increase in prevalence rates for children with ASD (e.g., Kogan et al., 2009). The use of the word *opportunity* is not used facetiously; there is much to be learned from teaching a young child with ASD. When you're open to the possibilities, teaching a child with ASD can enhance a classroom in many ways. In an effort to be conscientious about overgeneralizing to all children with ASD, the gifts are many. For example, their need for consistency and repetition highlights the developmentally appropriate concept of activity-based intervention (Bricker, Pretti-Frontczak, & McComas, 1998), which also incorporates routine-based teaching. In order to promote generalization of newly learned behaviors, a skill often lacking in students with ASD, routine teaching is ensured across multiple exemplars, settings, and teaching agents (Strain & Hoyson, 2000). Students with ASD teach one to become more cognizant of varied forms of communication, priming observation skills to become keenly aware of even the most subtle initiations from students, which creates more responsive teaching in classrooms. And lastly, individuals with ASD perceive the world through such a creative lens that by taking the time to share their views, one will most certainly gain insight full of greater depth and compassion. As with all children, respect for their beautiful gifts and unique strengths and challenges should be a central focus. Embracing this perspective will enhance the ability to see the child beyond the label of ASD.

Recommended Best Practices for Young Children With ASD

In 2001, the National Research Council (NRC) convened a panel of experts in the field of ASD to review the early intervention literature and develop a list of recommended practices that would enhance early childhood learning for children with ASD. These recommendations were developed from the available literature that was published at the time, which was primarily focused on children ages 3–5. Included in these recommended practices were the following: (1) intervention as soon as ASD is considered; (2) intensive programming with one-on-one and group-based teaching; (3) classrooms with low student-to-teacher ratio; (4) active family involvement; (5) appropriately trained staff; (6) ongoing and objective assessment of progress; (7) research-based teaching strategies; (8) critical learning goals; (9) facilitated interactions with typically developing peers; (10) individualized programs; and (11) transitions prepared in advance. The content included in this chapter expands upon these important recommendations raised by the NRC. It is intended to serve the preschool teacher and families of young children with ASD in identifying critical components to ensure successful outcomes for the preschool-aged student with ASD. These components are described under the following headings: (a) classroom considerations, (b) instructional strategies, (c) curriculum content, and (d) integration and inclusion practices.

Classroom Considerations

Early Intervention

Emerging research has demonstrated that the sooner children enter high-quality early intervention, the better the chance for positive outcomes (Harris & Handleman, 2000; NRC, 2001; Rogers & Dawson, 2010). Therefore, if a child displays autism characteristics, it is imperative to seek a diagnostic evaluation with a professional who specializes in ASD. Due to the fact that early signs and symptoms of ASD are quite complicated and oftentimes subtle, it is recommended that a specialist be involved who can thoroughly evaluate your child and make appropriate recommendations.

The second NRC recommendation includes the need for "intensive programming." This recommendation has been interpreted many ways and has placed a strain on the early intervention systems, which are responsible for delivering this intensive intervention (Schwartz & Sandall, 2010). However, it is important to take note that the original intention associated with this recommendation not only addressed the specific number of hours of intervention, but, more importantly, also stressed the quality and characteristic of the learning opportunities being provided. Strain and Hoyson (2000) endorsed the inclusion of a "large number of functional, developmentally relevant, and high-interest opportunities to respond actively" (p. 119). This notion emphasizes the importance of providing not only direct instruction, but also purposeful opportunities for the child to have facilitated experience with being the initiator, as well as the responder. Specifically, children should have the opportunity to choose when and what they want to talk about (initiator), so they do not only serve the role of answering others (responder).

Class Dynamics and Ongoing Support for Teachers

This section will expand upon the NRC recommendations of student-to-teacher ratios, delivery of instruction, staffing and support, classroom environment, visual supports, and routines. In most cases, typical preschool classrooms offer a smaller teacher-to-student ratio. Many preschool students have not yet been exposed to a group-learning environment and, therefore, adequate individual attention and gradual introduction to the concept of learning within a small group is advisable. When educating young children with ASD, it is recommended that the ratio be no more than two children with ASD per adult in the classroom (NRC, 2001). This ratio allows for the inclusion of both one-on-one and small-group teaching. Young students with ASD can sometimes benefit from more systematic and direct teaching first (further described below in the instructional strategies section), before they are ready to learn more implicitly in a naturalistic or small-group learning environment. By including a lower student-to-teacher ratio, the provision of these additional learning environments is made more feasible.

Due to the complex nature of ASD, it is recommended that teachers and staff have appropriate training, ongoing consultation, and follow-up (NRC, 2001). It is not possible for teachers to solely participate in a full-day workshop or training and be adequately prepared to effectively teach students with ASD in their classrooms (NRC, 2001). Effective programming requires not only successful implementation of evidence-based practices, but also ongoing monitoring of children's skill development that guide programmatic decisions. Teachers need ongoing support for systematic analysis of their teaching behavior and student response. It is recommended that a trained and experienced autism specialist be regularly available to engage in problem solving and positive practice discussions with teachers (Stahmer, 2007).

As a final point, one is reminded of the need for teachers to model essential dispositions such as caring, cooperation, authenticity, and collaboration (Carr, Fauske, & Rushton, 2008). The value in this practice is documented in Copple and Bredekamp's (2009) latest edition of *Developmentally Appropriate Practice in Early Childhood Programs: Serving Children From Birth Through Age 8*, where the authors emphasized that the teacher's actions beyond the curriculum (including reactions and interactions with students) have the greatest impact in the classroom. Therefore, it is the classroom teacher's responsibility to create a culture of respect (by modeling the act of listening and valuing all students' perspectives, by giving ample and supported opportunities for all students to successfully participate, and by ensuring that kindness and compassion are constantly shown toward classmates), while fostering the appreciation for differences among students. The creation of a safe and positive learning environment will establish important philosophies from an early age that will continue to impact the future learning and social connections of all students.

Classroom Environment

The classroom environment may be arranged to systematically enhance participation of students with ASD. Principles related to structured teaching (Mesibov, Shea, & Shopler, 2004) developed by the TEACCH (Treatment and Education of Autistic and related Communication handicapped Children) program in North Carolina may be utilized to provide visual information related to the physical arrangement of the room, the sequence of activities, independent work, and learning task organization. For example, existing furniture in the classroom may be used to provide a visual arrangement of the different teaching areas. The delineation of different teaching spaces (e.g., play time, circle time, snack area) provides students with a clearer picture of what the expectations are for each of the various areas of the classroom. It also clearly designates space for individualized, one-on-one, small-, and large-group learning. Immediately upon entering the classroom, the visual structure provides a sense of orderliness that assists to calm and organize the student with ASD.

In addition to the physical arrangement of the room, specific opportunities should be created throughout the classroom to promote child initiations. Spontaneous child initiations have shown to be lacking in children with ASD (Koegel, Koegel, & Carter, 1999) and, therefore, opportunities for children with ASD to initiate must be planned and promoted. One way to do this is by "sabotaging" the environment with motivating toys and objects that are in sight, but out of reach, so that the child with ASD is required to communicate (either verbally or nonverbally) to someone else in order to receive access to the desired item. Another powerful means of promoting initiations is by only giving a child a small piece of a desired food item during snack time and keeping the remaining portions in sight, but out of reach. When promoting and reinforcing child initiations, it is imperative that the teacher is familiar with nonverbal and less obvious means of communication (e.g., reaching, eye contact, proximity) utilized by the child with ASD, so that these communication attempts are immediately acknowledged and reinforced. This immediate reinforcement will strengthen the child's awareness of the power of communication to control the world around him. Further discussion about alternative and augmentative communication systems is included below.

Visual Supports

The use of visual supports has been utilized in many ways to assist in the education of children with ASD (Hodgdon, 1995). Visuals are often used to supplement information that is provided verbally. Visual supports can be provided in the form of real objects (or miniature objects), laminated labels (such as a label from a can of corn), color photographs, black and white 2D line drawings (such as Mayer Johnson pictures from the Boardmaker© program), or printed and written words. They provide an ongoing stable cue that aids with predictability, comprehension, and expression.

The use of visuals to support transitions and enhance independence was initially utilized by the TEACCH program and is most commonly implemented through visual picture schedules (Schopler, Mesibov, & Hearsey, 1995). Visual picture schedules are typically pictures or objects (depending upon the symbolic capacity of the child) that represent each of the classroom activities. There are a variety of ways to format and utilize visual picture schedules, but the principles surrounding the benefit of incorporating them into the classroom are invariable. One effective example is to provide each child with her own picture schedule (with her picture at the top) displayed vertically in one central area of the room. Prior to the change in activity, the transition should consistently be noted (e.g., ringing of a bell, using a timer, singing of a transition song), and children should be advised to check their schedules. Each schedule should have small 2-inch x 4-inch picture symbols (or objects) representing the next activity that can be detached by the child, taken to the next area of the room where the activity will occur, and matched (or attached) to a larger picture representing the same activity. This format provides a concrete representation of the transition and a physical guide to the next location. It also visually prepares the student for what is coming next through matching the smaller symbol to the larger one. Visual picture schedules reinforce daily routines, support transitions between activities and locations, assist the student in anticipating future events/activities, provide organization, and foster independence. When students feel organized in their learning environments, anxiety is reduced, and they can focus on the content of learning instead of the uncertainty of what is coming next. Figure 4.1 shows an example of such a schedule.

Figure 4.1. Example of a picture schedule.

Routines

Routines are additional ways to cultivate learning and familiarity. Because many children with ASD have difficulty with transitions and independently understanding the sequence of events and order of typical daily activities, the development of consistent routines within specific activities are beneficial. Fortunately, a considerable portion of the preschool curriculum is the establishment of routines (Nielson, 2006). This benefits the student with ASD immensely by providing repetitious exposure to consistent activities day after day in the classroom.

Routines can be used to not only establish the sequence of activities to be completed in the classroom, but also to promote learning. Snyder-McLean, Solomonson, McLean, and Sack (1984) adapted Bruner's (1975) concept of joint action routines for use as a naturalistic strategy to provide structure and predictable roles in order to promote mutual participation for children with language impairments. Joint action routines are common routines with clear roles and sequential steps. They can easily be incorporated into play activities to help create more clarity for the child with ASD in understanding the sequence of what will happen and what he is supposed to do. One example of a joint action routine is children reenacting going to the grocery store in play. In this joint action routine, the two roles would be "shopper" and "checker." The role of the shopper is to collect and pay for the food. Sequential steps consist of: (1) drive to store, (2) select the food, (3) go to checkout, (4) pay for the food, and (5) go home. The role of the checker is to: (1) gather the food, (2) ring up the food, (3) place the food in a bag, and (4) collect the money. The play routine requires joint activity between the two roles and provides for opportunities for specific events related to this routine to be modeled and prompted. Specific opportunities for related vocabulary are built into the routine. To encourage successful and continued learning, this play routine should be repeated and the roles should be reversed. The use of joint action routines in the preschool classroom, especially during play, scaffolds the expectations and requirements of a novel and unpredictable environment.

It is essential that small changes be incrementally introduced once the routines have been established. Not only is this important for children with ASD because of the potential for their resistance to change, but it is also a well-documented fact that a small dose of novelty must be introduced in order for learning to occur (Rushton, Juola-Rushton, & Larkin, 2010).

Instructional Strategies

This section will discuss the importance of developing a functional communication system for each child in the classroom, the importance of using evidence-based strategies in teaching, and the integration of various instructional strategies in the preschool classroom.

Functional Communication Systems

Given the significant impairment in the communication system of individuals with ASD (Kjelgaard & Tager-Flusberg, 2001), the need to establish a functional means for every student to communicate and participate in the classroom must be a top priority. Young children with ASD show impairments in both their nonverbal (gestures) and verbal communication systems (Wetherby & Prutting, 1984). Early communication patterns show a delay in the development of gestures, speech, and the means of communication (Wetherby et al., 2004). Children with ASD will often communicate to make their needs known (such as making requests for objects), but not for social purposes (such as greetings or shared attention).

When a child's communication system is impoverished, the child needs to be given an alternative or augmentative means to communicate functionally. Providing a child with ASD with such a system will also decrease the likelihood that he will learn to communicate through behaviors that interfere with learning (e.g., tantrums, aggression). There are a variety of ways young children may communicate without speaking including, but not limited to, sign language and gestures, use of pictures, the Picture Exchange Communication System (Bondy & Frost, 1994), and alternative and augmentative communication (AAC) devices. The communication system used will vary from child to child, but it is critical that the classroom teacher work with a speech-language pathologist and the family to determine which alternative means of communication will be most appropriate for the individual child. Once the alternative communication system has been established, the child must be taught how to use it, both to initiate communication and to respond to initiations from others. It is equally important that all persons with whom the child will be interacting in every environment be taught how to communicate using the alternative system. The new communication system must be available to the child in every environment and for use in each activity throughout the day.

Evidence-Based Practices and Integration of Instructional Strategies

It is clear that the field of early intervention for young children with ASD is still evolving and in need of more controlled research to demonstrate the efficacy of intervention practices (Rogers & Vismara, 2008). Two simultaneous events have shaped the practices that are deemed "best practice" in early intervention for children with ASD. In 2001, the No Child Left Behind Act (NCLB) was passed, which included a number of standard-based principles of education reform. One of the standards in NCLB emphasized an increase in quality of education by utilizing scientifically based research practices. At the same time, the NRC (2001) reviewed the literature on early intervention in ASD and recommended the use of evidence-based practices for the teaching of young children with ASD.

Odom, Boyd, Hall, and Hume (2010) recently published a report on the currently available evidence-based practices for teaching young children with ASD. Although one instructional strategy has not yet proven to be more effective at teaching young children with ASD than any other (NRC, 2001), the inclusion of a variety of complimentary intervention strategies have a promising effect on early development (Dawson et al., 2010; Landa, Holman, Stuart, & O'Neil, 2010; Stahmer, Ingersoll, & Koegel, 2004). The principles of applied behavior analysis (ABA) and descriptions of various instructional strategies were reviewed in Chapter 3; as a result, the remainder of this section will discuss the importance of using and integrating a variety of strategies into the teaching context.

Research has shown that children with ASD have difficulty learning implicitly (by imitation; Rogers & Pennington, 1991) and benefit from more explicit teaching. Given the heterogeneous nature of ASD, the integration of both types of teaching will ensure that all children respond and that the skills learned are effectively generalized to multiple contexts. For example, a teacher may begin teaching a child to imitate in a one-on-one discrete trial format, where the teaching is typically teacher directed and taught explicitly at a table outside of the natural environment. Once this skill has been established in this setting, it is imperative that imitation continues to be targeted in the natural environment (e.g., in play), using a more child-directed approach such as Pivotal Response Teaching (PRT; Koegel et al., 1999). This will allow the teacher to capitalize on the child's motivation and use of the skill spontaneously in more incidental learning environments such as play or circle time. The need for teachers to be well trained and to understand the importance of utilizing a variety of instructional strategies to effectively teach young children with ASD is something that must be facilitated by someone with expertise in ASD.

Curriculum Content

The intent of this section of the chapter is to indicate particular content areas to be included and focused upon when teaching a young student with ASD. Three specific content areas will be discussed below: (a) developmentally appropriate content, (b) fostering social and emotional development, and (c) communicating, collaborating, and empowering families.

Developmentally Appropriate Content

There is no denying the importance of early learning experiences on the development of a young child's social-emotional, cognitive, and physical development (Copple & Bredekamp, 2009). It is the responsibility of the early educator to stimulate a young child's exploration, discovery, and connections between self, others, and the world around her. Because ASD is considered a systems disorder (Thelan & Smith, 1994)—which implies that various developmental systems (e.g., language, social-emotional, attention, perception, cognition, motor/sensory) are affected in students with ASD—careful consideration of how to integrate information so that processing occurs through multiple domains is essential. It is crucial that the teacher, with prior knowledge, design the learning environment to be enriching and enticing in order to promote children's active exploration and connection between the various materials, toys, and learning opportunities. Three strategies to promote this type of learning include incorporation of multisensory teaching, integration of learning events, and repetition and frequent opportunities to use the skills that have been learned.

Students with ASD sometimes fail to utilize all of the environmental cues available to them, often focusing on or responding to irrelevant cues. This impairment in learning is often referred to as "stimulus overselectivity" (Lovaas, Schreibman, Koegel, & Rehm, 1971). For example, if you show a student a picture of a dog and label it verbally, he or she may hear the auditory cue of the word "dog," but instead of looking at the visual picture of the dog, he or she may be focusing on a tiny imprint of a staple in the corner of the paper. Multisensory teaching incorporates the use of two or more sensory modalities to simultaneously take in or express information (Slingerland, 1977). This will aid the comprehension of students with ASD by giving them multiple ways to take in or perceive information about the world around them. Other strategies for including multisensory teaching include tactile exploration of materials while describing them verbally and integrating movement into learning. For example, after reading the popular early childhood book *Brown Bear, Brown Bear, What Do You See?* by Bill Martin Jr. and Eric Carle, children could be invited to go on a "bear hunt" throughout the room by completing a specified obstacle course that involves crawling through tunnels and climbing up and down stairs in search of the visual pictures of the various animals just read about in the book. This type of active learning opportunity engages the prefrontal cortex of the brain and incorporates the visual, auditory, motor, cognitive, and perceptual systems, making learning more integrated and solidified (Rushton et al., 2010).

Another way to build multisensory integration is to utilize theme-based teaching, a familiar concept for early childhood education. The use of themes creates a framework for understanding in which concepts may be made salient and integrated throughout all learning opportunities (Christie & Enz, 1992). Themes typically utilized in early childhood classrooms are focused on concepts that are engaging and relevant for young children. By building upon these interests and applicable life experiences, the knowledge and skills are developed in meaningful ways. Inquiry and communication are activated by a desire to know more, resulting in increased participation in the learning process. The incorporation of special interests of children with ASD (Baker, Koegel, & Koegel, 1998) into this thematic learning network will enhance motivation and, therefore, improve the acquisition of skills and learning (Koegel & Koegel, 1995).

Utilizing the thematic framework provides a more comprehensive and systematic guide that requires the teacher to plan in advance to create individualized opportunities for the child to engage with the concepts during multiple activities throughout the day (Gardner, Wissick, Schweder, & Canter, 2003). This advanced planning also requires the teacher to incorporate theme-based materials that are engaging and promote active learning opportunities for children. It is not enough to simply fill the room with theme-related materials— specific learning opportunities must be planned and facilitated. One specific type of material that may be created to assist with active learning and concept development is adapted books. The teacher chooses developmentally appropriate early childhood literature and adapts the book to provide hands-on experiences with the targeted concepts. Using the prior example of *Brown Bear, Brown Bear, What Do You See?*, the teacher would choose one concept from each page to make salient by creating a smaller Boardmaker version of the concept with a single picture and a word such as *bear*. This picture would be laminated and attached to the book so that when instructed, the student would identify the picture of the bear, remove it from the page and match it to another larger picture of the bear attached to the wall.

The use of theme-based teaching also provides a systematic way for educators to organize repeated experiences with the specific concepts being taught. When students are provided with numerous opportunities to use the skills that they are learning, the connections between the concept being taught and the application of this concept within the classroom and beyond are strengthened (Rushton et al., 2010).

Fostering Social and Emotional Development

The preschool classroom has always been a rich landscape for the nurturing of social and emotional development. It is this age where social awareness peaks, and peer negotiations are cultivated. For the young student with ASD, who in many cases demonstrates a very different early trajectory of social and emotional development (Howlin, Goode, Hutton, & Rutter, 2004; Landa, Holman, & Garret-Meyer, 2007), direct attention and intercession of these developmental areas are imperative. Numerous studies have documented impairments in social referencing, joint attention (shared attention with another person around an object, activity, or an event), imitation, and shared affect in young children with ASD (Charman et al., 1997; Landa et al., 2007; Rogers, Hepburn, Stackhouse, & Wehner, 2003; Wetherby, Watt, Morgan, & Shumway, 2007). Conversely, several early intervention studies have demonstrated improvement in these skills for young children with ASD when they are directly targeted (Landa et al., 2010; Rocha, Schreibman, & Stahmer, 2007; Rogers & Dawson, 2010). This growing body of early intervention research provides the preschool teacher with specific tools that may be naturally incorporated into the classroom to not only nurture, but also directly promote the development of these crucial early social and emotional domains. In a study by Landa and colleagues (2010), the impact of a supplementary curriculum on the development of interpersonal synchrony (the ability to successfully interact reciprocally and socially with another person) of toddlers with ASD was evaluated. The researchers found that when critical elements of synchronous behavior, such as targeted joint attention, shared affect, and socially engaged imitation, were embedded into the typical preschool curriculum, there was a significant improvement of the toddlers' use of these interpersonal skills not readily present in young children with ASD (Landa et al., 2010).

The importance of creating a classroom that is rich in shared experiences centered on motivating objects and activities for all children cannot be emphasized enough. The supplementary interpersonal synchrony curriculum referred to above (Landa et al., 2010) provides an integrated framework for creating opportunities to promote social engagement and reciprocal interactions among young children in a classroom environment. Teachers who incorporate this curriculum into their classroom will learn to focus on creating many motivating opportunities for children to use these social skills throughout every activity in the classroom. The use of specific hierarchies and relevant activities related to the promotion of these early social abilities creates a positive impact on their development. It is critical to build these repertoires of social behavior early, so that they will create a strong foundation for continued development and positive impact on future social relationships. However, it is also important to recognize that genuine social interactions are not built on the learning of discrete skills alone (Strain & Schwartz, 2001), but also upon the nurturing of relationships within meaningful activities where these social behaviors can be facilitated, practiced, and naturally reinforced.

Communicating, Collaborating, and Empowering Families

When one is teaching the young child, it is essential to remember that this child is part of a larger family system (Turnbull & Turnbull, 2006). In their book, *Families, Professionals, and Exceptionality: Collaborating for Empowerment*, the Turnbulls (2006) described the seven principles of partnership. These principles—communication, professional competence, respect, trust, commitment, equality, and advocacy—create stepping stones that form a solid foundation for the relationships we build with the families of our students. Teachers need to understand the impact that raising a child with ASD has on the family. These unique factors include, but are not limited to, the following:

- scarcity of professionals who are adequately trained to teach their child;

- sometimes difficult to develop initial social bond;

- some children may show extensive behaviors in public, but they do not display any overt physical features;

- so many unknowns: unknown etiology, unspecific diagnosis, ASD is difficult to diagnose early, prognosis is difficult to predict, future is unknown; and

- the many claims of a "cure" that have been introduced to families, only to later be proven uneffective.

Families report being incredibly overwhelmed by the amount of information related to ASD (Cassidy, McConkey, Truesdale-Kennedy, & Slevin, 2008) and, therefore, it is the early childhood educator's responsibility to be knowledgeable regarding ASD and related services and interventions so that this information may be accurately shared with families. Dunst and Trivette (1988) reported that the most effective way to support families is by providing them with enough information to access needed resources, make informed decisions about their child's education, and maintain a sense of self-competence. Families need empirically sound information and guidance in interpreting this information in relation to their own child, so they can become empowered to be their child's best advocate for the journey ahead. As a preschool teacher, there are numerous ways to support and empower families. Figure 4.2 provides a list of suggestions.

Suggestions for Empowering Families of Children With ASD in Your Preschool Classroom

- Develop a parent training or education group (where various information about what autism is and hands-on training in how to facilitate a child's development is provided).
- Hold a specific "parent orientation" for your classroom to meet each parent and introduce him or her to your classroom and classroom policies.
- Connect parents with others by creating a "Parent Mentor Program" for new parents.
- Develop a community resource guide for your families to share with them at orientation, which may be accomplished through several different mediums:
  - paper/notebook,
  - link to class blog,
  - wiki (e.g., PB Works, Wikispace), or
  - internal website or sharepoint.

- Develop an effective and preferred method for communicating regularly with all families.
- Develop a questionnaire to give parents to complete about their child, family, and their needs/priorities. Then send a follow-up questionnaire about how parents are feeling about your communication and their child's progress halfway through and at the end of the school year.
- Videotape each child throughout the course of one day and invite families to meet with you to review the tape and see how their child is responding in the classroom.
- Create a resource notebook or library on autism that you keep in class and update regularly for parents to peruse/check out.
- Develop a monthly parent information night where you invite different professionals to speak about different areas of development or resources.
- Facilitate parents' connection to other families of children with disabilities through a parent network.
- Share information about (and attend when possible) local autism support groups. The Autism Society of America website includes a list of local support groups: http://209.200.89.252/search_site

Figure 4.2. **Tips for empowering parents.**

Inclusion and Integrated Practices

There are a variety of educational models for students with disabilities, and these models vary depending on what the IEP team has determined to be the least restrictive environment (LRE). This decision implies that the student is educated among typically developing peers to the greatest extent in which the individual student's learning can still be supported. Students with ASD are educated in a variety of settings including, but not limited to, a segregated program in an nonpublic or private school; a segregated classroom that is within a public school setting; partial inclusion within a public school setting (e.g., the student's primary educational placement is in a segregated special education classroom, but a portion of his time is spent with typical peers); reverse inclusion classroom (where typically developing students are educated within the segregated classroom for a portion or all of the day); or full inclusion with various levels of support (where a student with ASD is educated in a typical classroom for the entire day). The utilization of these different educational or inclusive models is discussed with respect to the different age groups in this book. The focus of this section will be a brief review of empirically validated inclusive preschool models, how to effectively foster peer relationships, and strategies for successful inclusion of a student with ASD among typically developing peers in the preschool setting.

Inclusive Preschool Models

There are two inclusive preschool models that have been empirically validated for young children with ASD: the Learning Experiences: An Alternative Program for Preschoolers and Parents program (LEAP; Kohler, Strain, Hoyson, & Jamieson, 1997) and the Walden Preschool program (McGee, Morrier, & Daly, 2001). Both models provide insight into important characteristics of effective programming for the successful inclusion of typically developing preschoolers and those with ASD including: (a) individualization of goals and objectives; (b) use of empirically validated teaching practices (e.g., peer-mediated strategies [Strain & Kohler, 1998], incidental teaching [McGee, Almeida, Sulzer-Azaroff, & Feldman, 1992]; (c) importance of data-driven programming; and (d) planned and frequent opportunities for instruction and facilitated social interactions. These models provide a comprehensive approach for successful inclusion and effective programming.

Facilitating Early Social Relationships

Regardless of an individual with ASD's language or cognitive ability, social abilities are pervasively impaired (Carter, Davis, Klin, & Volkmar, 2005). It is essential that emphasis is placed on fostering social development from an early age. This can begin in infancy through the child and caregiver dyad, extending through family members, and growing into peer relationships. Children with ASD do not develop social relationships or improve interaction and play skills simply by being around typically developing peers; shared opportunities for students to interact must be planned into the curriculum and specific positive interpersonal skills must be facilitated for both typically developing students and students with ASD (see Strain & Schwartz, 2001, for a review of behaviorally based social interventions).

It is important; however, to remember that the preschool-aged child is just beginning to move beyond parallel play with another child into a more meaningful interactive relationship. Therefore, the social interactive expectations of students with ASD need to be carefully aligned with what is developmentally appropriate for each child and not beyond what one would expect of a typically developing 3–5-year-old. That being said, the role of the preschool environment is to foster and nurture these early social relationships, providing opportunities for shared experiences and practice using skills such as conflict negotiation, affect and toy sharing, and empathy. Several models have been utilized as frameworks for including older students with ASD and building social relationships: peer networks (Kamps, Potucek, Lopez, Kravits, & Kemmerer, 1997), peer tutoring and cooperative groups, and integrated play groups (Wolfberg & Schuler, 1999). This last model is one that has been utilized with preschool-aged children and is a promising format for providing ongoing and facilitated support for children with ASD to play and interact with typically developing peers.

Wolfberg and Schuler (1999) developed the integrated playgroups model based on Vygotsky's perspective of play as a social activity. The strategy of "guided participation" in play refers to an adult or teacher assisting novice and expert players to interact together and engage in more complex play actions. The terms *novice* and *expert* refer to the child's competencies in play. The goal is for the novice player to obtain more advanced play repertoires through guided interactions with the expert players. The primary objectives are to facilitate mutually enjoyed and reciprocal play among children while expanding novice players' social and symbolic repertoires. Since its original conception, this model has been developed into a very user-friendly field manual (Wolfberg, 2003) that can be easily adapted and incorporated into a typical preschool setting during play portions of the day.

Tips for Successful Inclusion

Educational inclusion refers to a set of practices and beliefs about how best to support individuals with disabilities in the educational setting where students who are typically developing learn. The successful inclusion of a student with a disability within the regular education classroom requires not only the implementation of strategies that have been empirically supported to enhance the process, but also the utilization of individualized decision making regarding supports, strengths, and academic and social needs (Fuchs & Fuchs, 1994). A responsive and successful inclusive classroom will provide the supportive environment necessary to encourage the physical, emotional, social, and cognitive development of all students. Please see the section on inclusion in Chapter 5 or Figure 4.3 for suggestions on successfully including the preschool student with ASD.

Conclusion

One looks back with appreciation to the brilliant teachers, but with gratitude to those who touched our human feelings. The curriculum is so much necessary material, but warmth is the vital element for the growing plant and for the soul of the child.

Carl Jung

It is understandable to feel somewhat overwhelmed by the amount

---

Successfully Including the Preschool Student With ASD

Successful inclusion requires:
- cultivation of respect and acceptance for differences among all students;
- implementation of universal design for learning and differentiation of instruction practices within the developmentally appropriate curriculum;
- utilization of evidence-based practices to promote both academic and social growth;
- incorporation of visuals and additional materials that support the learning of the student with ASD;
- integration of ongoing support and training from an expert in ASD;
- utilization of data monitoring systems to inform teaching practices;
- collaboration with other professionals through coplanning, coteaching, sharing of resources, and frequent communication about the successes and needed modifications; and
- partnership with parents in planning and evaluating meaningful learning experiences.

Figure 4.3. **Tips for including preschool students with ASD.**

---

of information that is required to effectively teach a student with ASD, however, the strategies and curriculum content suggestions described in this chapter are enhancements of the teaching practices that are inherent in most teachers. What is essential is the desire and compassion within that will make a true difference in the successful inclusion and education of the preschool student with ASD.

Tables 4.1 and 4.2 are checklists of the essential elements for an effective preschool classroom for a student with ASD from both a teacher's and parent's perspective.

Table 4.1

Essential Elements for an Effective Preschool Classroom for a Student With ASD (Teachers)

Arrangement of the Optimum Learning Environment	
Environmental Engineering	• TEACCH principles are incorporated to visually specify different teaching spaces using furniture and natural properties of the room. • Each of the different learning spaces, including areas for both one-on-one and group-based learning, is visually arranged and clearly designated. • Teachers implement planned location and storage (clear bins with lids) of toys and materials to promote spontaneous initiations from student. • The environment is arranged to facilitate learning and use of language (e.g., control of materials; arrangement of materials in sight, but out of reach).
Materials Inventory and Planned Use	• A materials inventory has been created to provide the teacher with an organized database of what materials are available for each unit and what needs to be created. • Teachers maximize the learning space by ensuring that there are a variety of developmentally appropriate and motivating toys and activities for all students. • Theme-related materials have been developed and how they will be used to engage children in activities has been specifically planned. • The teaching staff regularly brainstorms about different ways to utilize the toys in the play area in order to stimulate engaging and creative play ideas.
Planned Instruction	
Theme-Based Planning	• Lesson plans provide an integrated structure that reveals for teachers how much (or little) they are infusing theme-based concepts into every activity throughout the day.
Planned Teaching Opportunities	• Lesson plans include a variety of planned, motivating, effective teaching opportunities that systematically repeat important concepts throughout the learning day. • Goals targeted within each teaching opportunity are identified. For example, while reading stories, students will have the opportunity to identify pictures in the book (receptive vocabulary goal) and give objects to peers (social goal).
Comprehensive Curriculum	• Teachers use a comprehensive curriculum to collect initial student skill levels and assist with development of individual goals and regular monitoring of progress (some suggested preschool curricula include: Assessment, Evaluation, and Programming System for Infants and Children [AEPS; Bricker, 2002] and The Creative Curriculum for Preschool [Dodge, Colker, & Heroman, 2010]). • Teachers ensure that the curriculum includes (or supplements the curriculum with) activities that address the core deficits of social communication and interpersonal engagement (e.g., joint attention, social initiations, socially engaged imitation, shared affect) present in students with ASD.

Table 4.1, continued

Social Development and Social Interaction	
Social Development	• A student's social and emotional development is promoted. • The development of joint attention, social initiation, socially engaged imitation, and shared affect are directly targeted throughout all teaching opportunities. • Positive affect is consistently modeled and opportunities for engagement with others are planned into a variety of learning experiences.
Facilitated Social Interactions	• Classroom is filled with shared experiences that include motivating objects and activities for all children. • Multiple, planned, and frequent opportunities for instruction and adult-facilitated social interactions among all students are available, especially with typically developing peers and students with ASD. • Teachers use joint action routines to provide structure and predictable roles to promote mutual participation in social play for all students. • Play scripts or visual stories are used to support the play of students with ASD with their peers.
Effective Teaching Practices	
Functional Communication Systems	• Every student has a functional means of communicating, whether this is verbally; through gestures or sign language, pictures, or voice output devices; or a combination of the above. • Student uses his communication system independently to successfully communicate for a variety of reasons (e.g., needs and wants, social greeting, commenting). • Teachers model multimodal communication (e.g., incorporation of verbal words, signs, and pictures) to enhance the student's ability to comprehend others, communicate with others, and maximize participation and learning.
Visual Supports	• Visual supports are used in the classroom to enhance comprehension and provide concrete and static information to the student about a variety of concepts (e.g., visually adapted picture books, pictures, and printed words in various areas of the classroom to assist with clean up and organization). • Teachers use visual supports about what is happening next, what to do, and the expectations for a variety of environments or social contexts (e.g., visual picture schedules, visual social stories).
Sensory-Based Activities and Motor Routines	• A variety of sensory-based activities and motor routines are incorporated to provide the necessary input to assist with regulating the sensory system and optimize learning. This could be accomplished through a specific sensory area that includes multiple sensory-based experiences (e.g., sand and water table, mini slide and baby pool filled with plastic balls, a jump-o-lene) or by integrating sensory-based activities naturally throughout the day (e.g., use of sensory-motor routines when transitioning from one activity to the next, providing sensory-based alternatives for seating such as a bean bag chair or large bouncy ball)

Table 4.1, continued

Multisensory Teaching	• Multisensory teaching, which allows the student to explore objects or participate in activities using two or more sensory modalities (e.g., auditory and visual; motor, verbal, and sensory), is incorporated. See the description related to the *Brown Bear* book found within Chapter 4 for a more details.
Evidence-Based Instructional Strategies	• Instructional strategies that have been researched and proven to be beneficial in teaching students with ASD, often referred to as "evidence-based practices," are utilized. • A variety of evidence-based practices that include adult-led instruction in more controlled settings and child-led instruction within the natural environment are integrated. • Teachers use specific instructional strategies that are individualized to meet each student's unique learning needs. For example, a student who needs the concepts to be broken down into smaller units, who needs adult-directed repetitive practice, or who needs reinforcement that is not directly related to the concept may respond better to the direct instruction provided with Discrete Trial Teaching. In comparison, a student who independently imitates and learns more incidentally may respond better to child-led strategies, such as Pivotal Response Training, which can be implemented in natural play environments.
Data Collection and Progress Monitoring	• Effective and useful data collection systems are developed and used regularly to inform the teacher about individual student progress (at least every 3 months). • Ongoing and objective data analysis is conducted in order to determine when programs need to be modified to ensure continued learning and maximize outcomes.
Collaboration and Empowering Families	
Collaborating With Families	• Educators should partner with families and empower them by providing sound information that can be used to make informed decisions about their child's education. • Families should be actively involved in the education process, sharing input on goals, progress, and priorities.
Teacher Training and Ongoing Support	
Teacher Training	• Teachers should participate in training to learn how to adequately support the learning needs of students with ASD. • Ongoing support by professionals with extensive training in ASDs should be readily available.
Essential Dispositions	• Teachers should model essential dispositions of caring, cooperation, authenticity, and collaboration (see further description in the introduction and within Chapter 4). • Teachers should foster appreciation of differences among students. • Teachers should create a safe and positive learning environment in their classroom.

Table 4.2

Essential Elements for an Effective Preschool Classroom for a Child With ASD (Parents)

Arrangement of the Optimum Learning Environment	
Environmental Engineering and Materials	• When you walk into the classroom you can determine how the room is arranged for different teaching activities within the visually demarcated areas. • The classroom is filled with a variety of toys that appear to be age appropriate and motivating. • The toys are rotated regularly to preserve their novelty and selected based on their representation of the current teaching theme. For example, if the theme was "food," toys related to cooking and eating would be present; if the theme was "water," toys like a fishing set, boats, or sea creatures would be available. • Visual pictures and printed words are readily seen and posted throughout the classroom. • Theme-based materials (e.g., pictures related to the books read in class) and child-friendly materials are utilized in the classroom, but the amount of materials on the wall is not overdone as to be a distraction.
Planned Instruction	
Theme-Based Planning	• Information related to selected teaching themes are shared with parents and suggestions for carryover of teaching concepts at home are shared either verbally or through consistent and clearly written communication.
Comprehensive Curriculum	• A comprehensive curriculum is used to collect initial student skill levels and assist with development of individual goals and regular monitoring of progress. • The curriculum includes or is supplemented with activities that address the core deficits of social communication and interpersonal engagement (e.g., joint attention, social initiations, socially engaged imitation, shared affect) present in children with ASD.
Social Development and Social Interaction	
Social Development	• Teachers actively promote students' social and emotional development. • Teachers directly target the development of joint attention, social initiation, socially engaged imitation, and shared affect throughout all teaching opportunities. • Positive affect is consistently modeled and opportunities for engagement with others are planned into a variety of learning experiences.
Facilitated Social Interactions	• Classroom is filled with shared experiences that include motivating objects and activities for all children. • Teachers actively facilitate social interactions among all students, especially with typically developing peers and students with ASD. • Play scripts or visual stories are available to support the facilitated play of students with ASD with their peers.

Table 4.2, *continued*

Effective Teaching Practices	
Functional Communication Systems	• Every student has a functional means of communicating, whether this is verbally; through gestures or sign language, pictures, or voice output devices; or a combination of the above. • Student uses his communication system independently to successfully communicate for a variety of reasons (e.g., needs and wants, social greeting, commenting). • Teachers model multimodal communication (e.g., incorporation of verbal words, signs, and pictures) to enhance the student's ability to comprehend others, communicate with others, and maximize participation and learning.
Visual Supports	• Visual supports are used in the classroom to enhance comprehension and provide concrete and static information to the student about a variety of concepts (e.g., visually adapted picture books, pictures and printed words in various areas of the classroom to assist with clean up and organization). • Teachers use visual supports about what is happening next, what to do, and the expectations for a variety of environments or social contexts (e.g., visual picture schedules, visual social stories).
Sensory-Based Activities and Motor Routines	• A variety of sensory-based activities and motor routines are incorporated to provide the necessary input to assist with regulating the sensory system and optimize learning. This could be accomplished through a specific sensory area that includes multiple sensory-based experiences (e.g., sand and water table, mini slide and baby pool filled with plastic balls, a jump-o-lene) or by integrating sensory-based activities naturally throughout the day (e.g., use of sensory-motor routines when transitioning from one activity to the next, providing sensory-based alternatives for seating such as a bean bag chair or large bouncy ball).
Multisensory Teaching	• Multisensory teaching, which allows the student to explore objects or participate in activities using two or more sensory modalities (e.g., auditory and visual; motor, verbal, and sensory), is incorporated. See the description related to the *Brown Bear* book found within Chapter 4 for more details.
Evidence-Based Instructional Strategies	• Instructional strategies that have been researched and proven to be beneficial in teaching students with ASD, often referred to as "evidence-based practices," are utilized. • A variety of evidence-based practices that include adult-led instruction in more controlled settings and child-led instruction within the natural environment are integrated. • Teachers use specific instructional strategies that are individualized to meet each student's unique learning needs. For example, a student who needs the concepts to be broken down into smaller units, who needs adult-directed repetitive practice, or who needs reinforcement that is not directly related to the concept may respond better to the direct instruction provided with Discrete Trial Teaching. In comparison, a student who independently imitates and learns more incidentally may respond better to child-led strategies, such as Pivotal Response Training, which can be implemented in natural play environments.

Table 4.2, *continued*

Data Collection and Progress Monitoring	• Effective and useful data collection systems are used regularly to inform the teacher about individual student progress (at least every 3 months). • Ongoing and objective data analysis is conducted in order to determine when programs need to be modified to ensure continued learning and maximize outcomes.
Collaboration and Empowering Families	
Collaborating With Families	• Educators should partner with families and empower them by providing sound information that can be used to make informed decisions about their child's education. • Families should be actively involved in the education process, sharing input on goals, progress, and priorities.
Teacher Training and Ongoing Support	
Teacher Training	• Teachers should participate in training to learn how to adequately support the needs of students with ASD in the classroom. • Ongoing support by professionals with extensive training in ASDs should be readily available.
Essential Dispositions	• Teachers should model essential dispositions of caring, cooperation, authenticity, and collaboration (see further description in the introduction and within Chapter 4). • Teachers should foster appreciation of differences among students. • Teachers should create a safe and positive learning environment in their classrooms.

References

Baker, M., Koegel, R., & Koegel, L. (1998). Increasing the social behavior of young children with autism using their obsessive behaviors. *Journal of the Association for Persons with Severe Handicaps, 23,* 300–308. doi:10.2511/rpsd.23.4.300

Bondy, A. S., & Frost, L. A. (1994). The Picture Exchange Communication System. *Focus on Autistic Behavior, 9,* 1–19.

Bricker, D. (2002). *Assessment, evaluation, and programming system for infants and children: Birth to three years* (2nd ed.). Baltimore, MD: Brookes.

Bricker, D., Pretti-Frontczak, K., & McComas, N. (1998). *An activity-based approach to early intervention* (2nd ed.). Baltimore, MD: Brookes.

Bruner, J. (1975). The ontogenesis of speech acts. *Journal of Child Language, 2*(1), 1–19.

Carr, J., Fauske, J., & Rushton, S. (2008). *Teaching and leading from the inside out: A model for reflection, exploration, and action.* Thousand Oaks, CA: Corwin Press.

Carter, A., Davis, N., Klin, A., & Volkmar, F. (2005). Social development in autism. In F. R. Volkmar, R. Paul, A. Klin, & D. Cohen (Eds.), *Handbook of autism and pervasive developmental disorders* (2nd ed., pp. 312–334). Hoboken, NJ: Wiley.

Cassidy, A., McConkey, R., Truesdale-Kennedy, M., & Slevin, E. (2008). Preschoolers with autism spectrum disorders: The impact on families and the supports available to them. *Early Child Development and Care, 178,* 115–128.

Charman, T., Swettenham, J., Baron-Cohen, S., Cox, A., Baird, G., & Drew, A. (1997). Infants with autism: An investigation of empathy, pretend play, joint attention and imitation. *Developmental Psychology, 33,* 781–789.

Christie, J., & Enz, B. (1992). The effects of literacy play interventions on preschoolers' play patterns and literacy development. *Early Education and Development, 3,* 205–220.

Copple, C., & Bredekamp, S. (Eds.). (2009). *Developmentally appropriate practice in early childhood programs: Serving children from birth though age 8* (3rd ed.). Washington, DC: National Association for the Education of Young Children.

Dawson, G., Rogers, S., Munson, J., Smith, M., Winter, J., Greenson, J., & Varley, J. (2010). Randomized, controlled trial of an intervention for toddlers with autism: The Early Start Denver Model. *Pediatrics, 125,* e17–e23.

Dodge, D. T., Colker, L. J., & Heroman, C. (2010). *The creative curriculum for preschool* (5th ed.). Bethesda, MD: Teaching Strategies.

Dunst, C., & Trivette, C. (1988). Determinants of parent and child interactive behavior. *Parent-child interaction and developmental disabilities: Theory, research, and intervention* (pp. 3–31). New York, NY: Praeger.

Fuchs, D., & Fuchs, L. S. (1994). Inclusive schools movement and the radicalization of special education reform. *Exceptional Children, 60,* 294–309.

Gardner, J., Wissick, C., Schweder, W., & Canter, L. (2003). Enhancing interdisciplinary instruction in general and special education: Thematic units and technology. *Remedial and Special Education, 24,* 161–172.

Harris, S., & Handleman, J. (2000). Age and IQ at intake as predictors of placement for young children with autism: A four- to six-year follow-up. *Journal of Autism and Developmental Disorders, 30,* 137–142.

Hodgdon, L. Q. (1995). Solving social-behavioral problems through the use of visually supported communication. In K. A. Quill (Ed.), *Teaching children with autism: Strategies to enhance communication and socialization* (pp. 265–286). New York, NY: Delmar.

Howlin, P., Goode, S., Hutton, J., & Rutter, M. (2004). Adult outcome for children with autism. *Journal of Child Psychology and Psychiatry, 45,* 212–229.

Kamps, D. M., Potucek, J., Lopez, A. G., Kravits, T., & Kemmerer, K. (1997). The use of peer networks across multiple settings to improve social interaction for students with autism. *Journal of Behavioral Education, 7,* 335–357.

Kjelgaard, M. M., & Tager-Flusberg, H. (2001). An investigation of language impairment in autism: Implications for genetic subgroups. *Language and Cognitive Processes, 16,* 287–308.

Koegel, L., & Koegel, R. (1995). Motivating communication in children with autism. In E. Schopler & G. B. Mesibov (Eds.), *Learning and cognition in autism* (pp. 73–87). New York, NY: Plenum Press.

Koegel, R., Koegel, L., & Carter, C. (1999). Pivotal teaching interactions for children with autism. *School Psychology Review, 28,* 576–594.

Kogan, M. D., Blumbers, S. T., Schieve, L. A., Boyle, C. A., Perrin, J. M., Ghandour, R. M., . . . van Dyck, P. C. (2009). Prevalence of patient-reported diagnosis of autism spectrum disorder among children in the US, 2007. *Journal of the American Academy of Pediatrics, 124,* 1395–1403.

Kohler, F., Strain, P., Hoyson, M., & Jamieson, B. (1997). Merging naturalistic teaching and peer-based strategies to address the IEP objectives of preschoolers with autism: An examination of structural and child behavior outcomes. *Focus on Autism and Other Developmental Disabilities, 12,* 196–206.

Landa, R. J., Holman, K. C., & Garrett-Mayer, E. (2007). Social and communication development in toddlers with early and later diagnosis of autism spectrum disorders. *Archives of General Psychiatry, 64,* 853–864.

Landa, R., Holman, K. C., Stuart, E., & O'Neil, A. (2010). Intervention targeting development of socially synchronous engagement in toddlers with autism spectrum disorder: A randomized controlled trial. *Journal of Child Psychology and Psychiatry, 64,* 853–864.

Lovaas, O., Schreibman, L., Koegel, R., & Rehm, R. (1971). Selective responding by autistic children to multiple sensory input. *Journal of Abnormal Psychology, 77,* 211–222. doi:10.1037/h0031015

McGee, G. G., Almeida, M., Sulzer-Azaroff, B., & Feldman, R. S. (1992). Promoting reciprocal interactions via peer incidental teaching. *Journal of Applied Behavior Analysis, 25,* 117–126.

McGee, G. G., Morrier, M. J., & Daly, T. (2001). The Walden early childhood programs. In J. S. Handleman & S. L. Harris (Eds.), *Preschool education programs for children with autism* (2nd ed., pp. 157–190). Austin, TX: PRO-ED.

Mesibov, G. B., Shea, V., & Schopler, E. (2004). *The TEACCH approach to autism spectrum disorders.* New York, NY: Springer.

National Research Council. (2001). *Educating children with autism.* Washington, DC: National Academy Press.

Nielsen, D. (2006). *Teaching young children: A guide to planning your curriculum, teaching through learning centers, and just about everything else* (2nd ed.). Thousand Oaks, CA: Corwin Press.

No Child Left Behind Act, 20 U.S.C. §6301 (2001).

Odom, S., Boyd, B., Hall, L., & Hume, K. (2010). Evaluation of comprehensive treatment models for individuals with autism spectrum disorders. *Journal of Autism and Developmental Disorders, 40,* 425–436.

Rocha, M., Schreibman, L., & Stahmer, A. (2007). Effectiveness of training parents to teach joint attention to children with autism. *Journal of Early Intervention, 29,* 154–172.

Rogers, S., & Dawson, G. (2010). *Early Start Denver Model for young children with autism: Promoting language, learning, and engagement.* New York, NY: Guilford Press.

Rogers, S. J., Hepburn, S. L., Stackhouse, T., & Wehner, E. (2003). Imitation performance in toddlers with autism and those with other developmental disorders. *Journal of Child Psychology and Psychiatry, 44,* 763–781.

Rogers, S. J., & Pennington, B. (1991). A theoretical approach to the deficits in infantile autism. *Developmental Psychopathology, 2,* 137–162.

Rogers, S. J., & Vismara, L. A. (2008). Evidence-based comprehensive treatments for early autism. *Journal of Clinical Child and Adolescent Psychology, 37*, 8–38.

Rushton, S., Juola-Rushton, A., & Larkin, E. (2010). Neuroscience, play and early childhood education: Connections, implications, and assessment. *Early Childhood Education Journal, 37*, 351–361.

Schopler, E., Mesibov, G., & Hearsey, K. (1995). Structured teaching in the TEACCH system. In E. Shopler & G. Mesibov (Eds.), *Learning and cognition in autism* (pp. 243–268). New York, NY: Plenum Press.

Schwartz, I., & Sandall, S. (2010). Is autism the disability that breaks Part C? A commentary on "Infants and toddlers with autism spectrum disorder: Early identification and early intervention," by Boyd, Odom, Humphreys, and Sam. *Journal of Early Intervention, 32*, 105–109.

Slingerland, B. (1977). *A multi-sensory approach to language arts for specific language disability children.* Cambridge, MA: Educators Publishing Services.

Snyder-McLean, L., Solomonson, B., McLean, J., & Sack, S. (1984). Structuring joint action routines: A strategy for facilitating communication and language development in the classroom. *Seminars in Speech and Language, 5*, 213–228.

Stahmer, A. S. (2007). The basic structure of community early intervention programs for children with autism: Provider descriptions. *Journal of Autism and Developmental Disorders, 37*, 1344–1354.

Stahmer, A., Ingersoll, B., & Koegel, R. (2004). Inclusive programming for toddlers with autism spectrum disorders: Outcomes from the Children's Toddler School. *Journal of Positive Behavior Interventions, 6*, 67–82.

Strain, P. S. (1991). Ensuring quality of early intervention for children with severe disabilities. In L. Meyer, C. A. Peck, & L. Brown (Eds.), *Critical issues in the lives of people with severe disabilities* (pp. 479–483). Baltimore, MD: Brookes.

Strain, P., & Hoyson, M. (2000). The need for longitudinal, intensive social skill intervention: LEAP follow-up outcomes for children with autism. *Topics in Early Childhood Special Education, 20*, 116–122.

Strain, P. S., & Kohler, F. W. (1998). Peer-mediated social intervention for young children with autism. *Seminars in Speech and Language, 19*, 391–405.

Strain, P. S., & Schwartz, I. (2001). ABA and the development of meaningful social relations for young children with autism. *Focus on Autism and Other Developmental Disabilities, 16,* 120–128.

Thelan, E., & Smith, L. B. (1994). *A dynamic systems approach to the development of cognition and action.* Cambridge, MA: MIT Press.

Turnbull, A. P., & Turnbull, H. R. (2006). *Families, professionals, and exceptionality: Collaborating for empowerment* (5th ed.). Columbus, OH: Merrill.

Wetherby, A., & Prutting, C. (1984). Profiles of communicative and cognitive-social abilities in autistic children. *Journal of Speech and Hearing Research, 27,* 364–377.

Wetherby, A. M., Watt, N., Morgan, L., & Shumway, S. (2007). Social communication profiles of children with autism spectrum disorders late in the second year of life. *Journal of Autism and Developmental Disorders, 37,* 960–975.

Wetherby A. M., Woods, J., Allen, L., Cleary, J., Dickinson, H., & Lord, C. (2004). Early indicators of autism spectrum disorder in the second year of life. *Journal of Autism and Developmental Disorders, 34,* 473–493.

Wolfberg, P. (2003). *Peer play and the autism spectrum: The art of guiding children's socialization and imagination.* Shawnee Mission, KS: Autism Asperger.

Wolfberg, P., & Schuler, A. (1999). Fostering peer interaction, imaginative play and spontaneous language in children with autism. *Child Language Teaching and Therapy, 15,* 41–52.

chapter 5

Successful Elementary Programs for Students With Autism Spectrum Disorders[1]

Sara G. Egorin-Hooper

No matter how concerned you are about mankind
as a whole, you must never overlook the individual.
Every human being is a world in himself!

Elie Wiesel

E A C H unique student with ASD in an elementary classroom needs to feel affirmed, engaged, and supported by all teachers and staff members with whom he is working and growing. Remarkable teachers see infinite possibilities in their students, look to continually deepen their understanding, and refine, enhance, and improve learning environments, instruction, and curricula. As this chapter explores the realm of elementary programs for students with

1 Sincere gratitude to the following amazing people for their continual support, reflection, and feedback while developing this chapter: Susie Swindell, Chris Swanson, Paula Simon, Patty Meijer, Donna Gosnell, Melissa Keller, Michele Conneely, Amanda Hauf, and Cindi Manger.

ASD, it will examine important classroom considerations, significant instructional strategies and supports, noteworthy curriculum content considerations, and effective inclusive practices.

The fundamental and concrete ideas in each section of the chapter lay a foundation for a wide array of additional concepts that acknowledge and respond to each student as a whole human being with a learning profile of special, individual strengths and needs. Due to space limitations, many of these foundational issues are only introduced and the reader is provided with references for further reading and understanding. The intent for all students is to enable them to see the joy and purpose in learning, to be active contributors and valued members of the classroom, and to be presented with challenging, yet attainable learning opportunities.

Classroom Considerations

"You can never be too _____ or too _____."

For those who have experience in working with students ASD, they would suggest that the blanks in the sentence above should be completed with the following words: *structured, predictable, consistent, routine,* and *familiar.* They recognize that establishing a classroom where students with ASD feel safe and orderly is about creating comfort through familiarity. This notion leads to the all-important question:

> "If I were the student, what would I want the teacher and staff to do to help me to feel a sense of comfort and order both internally and externally so that I can be my best and achieve the most?"

Through the eyes of students with ASD, entering an unfamiliar classroom for which they are unprepared would be as if a visitor arrives at an exciting, loud, crowded festival with no map, no schedule of events, and no idea of how to maneuver and negotiate the myriad people, events, opportunities, and experiences. What occurs to the visitor instead is an overwhelming, chaotic, and anxiety-producing event in which the visitor feels lost and alone and reflects these feelings through actions. These same negative emotions are exactly what will be evoked and observed when the teacher does not take responsibility and action to establish order, structure, and clear boundaries in a classroom for students with ASD. Creating a structured, predictable environment increases the likelihood that students with ASD will initiate and respond successfully during learning activities, demonstrate more flexibility in responding, and function more independently.

There are numerous factors that a teacher should consider when developing and implementing successful elementary classroom programs for students with ASD. In this section of the chapter, specific classroom considerations are reviewed that will create optimum comfort and order for students with ASD.

Student-to-Adult Ratio

The ratio of 6 students to 3 staff members (one teacher and two paraeducators) is recommended so that sound, exemplary instruction can take place (National Research Council, 2001). A rotation system should be employed to provide individual teacher time, independent work time, and small-group instruction. To effectively implement this system, well-trained, dependable adults must be in each specific area of the classroom to facilitate student learning. Students with ASD who are being educated outside of the general education classroom will have the need for a more focused, intensive, and specialized instructional program by the very nature of this more restrictive placement.

Effective Collaboration With Related Service Providers

It is ideal to have related service providers who have an in-depth knowledge of the students in the classroom serve as collaborative teaching partners and consultants. Classroom staff can observe the implementation of programs and are more likely to integrate them into the students' daily routines. This model allows supports to be provided in a more authentic context and thus lends itself to generalization of student responses.

Home-School Communication

Each teacher needs to see the family as a partner in the student's education. Family members can provide insights, perspectives, and options of which educators may not otherwise be aware. Often educators spend a great amount of time looking for solutions and strategies that families may have already successfully or unsuccessfully tried. Additionally, many families want to reinforce skills, concepts, and behaviors as well as prepare students for upcoming learning and events. It is imperative that a mutually agreed upon consistent home-school communication system be in place. This can be as simple as daily notes in a notebook, a daily communication form, or a checklist that indicates activities, meals, skills, and special events addressed or occurring that day.

Visually Defined Boundaries and Areas

As teachers plan for having students with autism, they must consider what activities the students will participate in each day, where each of those activities will take place, and the pacing and timing of instruction for individual needs. Having a well-labeled, consistent location for each specific activity reinforces the sense of comfort and order that is essential for students with ASD. All classroom areas should be arranged so as to allow the staff to effectively supervise, monitor, and direct students at all times.

Teachers should establish clearly delineated areas for adult-student (one-to-one) work time, independent student work tasks, whole-group and small-group work, play/leisure time, sensory/motor activities, and transitions. The physical layout of the classroom should provide the structure to support students with ASD by focusing their attention on the expected tasks and behaviors associated with each area and the relationship between scheduled activities. A transition area should be established that contains the individual student schedules where students go before and between each task to review their schedule and to learn what the next activity will be.

Classroom Schedules

Teachers should establish structure for students with ASD by making use of and teaching students to follow daily class and individual schedules. The daily class schedule posted for all to see should have visual supports such as photographs or picture symbols to enhance the understanding of all students. The schedule should be reviewed on a daily basis with students in the morning and as needed in the afternoon and should reflect any changes such as field trips and special events, with a clear explanation in advance to prepare students for an altered schedule.

The example in Table 5.1 details a daily class schedule based on a class of six students and three adults. Although it is important to work within a consistent routine, it is equally important to alternate the format of each task/activity within the lessons. For example, teachers should alternate seatwork with more kinesthetic learning activities and alternate group work with more independent and individual instruction. Any schedule should be developed with the student's skill level in mind. For example, many students with ASD will require visual pictures or symbols in addition to written words, while other students may require only written words if they read with comprehension.

Individual schedules are an essential part of classroom structure that help students with ASD understand the sequence of events throughout their day, anticipate and predict activities to reduce anxiety and decrease frustration related to not knowing what to expect, or look forward to preferred activities. The individual student schedules may use words with or without photographs or visual symbols based on unique student abilities. Staff should keep in mind, however, that although many students with ASD are strong readers, visual supports

Table 5.1

Sample Daily Classroom Schedule

Time	Activity	Details
8:30–8:45	Arrival activities	Students unpack and follow the arrival routine; start morning work activities.
8:45–9:15	Morning Circle (whole group)	Social greetings, attendance for recognition and counting, calendar, schedule, and weather. Students alternate leading different activities.
9:15–10:00	Reading Work Rotations	Rotations: Independent work activities; one-on-one teacher time; small group; and centers (computer center, listening center, and/or sensory center). This is an ideal time for speech therapy, occupational therapy (OT), or physical therapy (PT) services to be delivered.
10:00–10:15	Physical Activity (whole group)	Yoga, group walk, or motor circuit activities. Movement and music activities from literature themes can be incorporated during this time.
10:15–11:00	Math Work Rotations	Rotations: Independent work activities; one-on-one teacher time; small group; centers (computer center, listening center, and/or sensory center). This is an ideal time for speech, OT, or PT services to be delivered.
11:00–11:20	Break Time (whole group)	Bathroom/hygiene. Snack time: social skills, communication, functional/life skills, manners.
11:20–11:50	Related Arts	Art, music, P.E., library, or technology class
11:50–12:20	Group Activities (Alternate throughout the week)	Choice making for games, songs, books, and video clips with peer buddies from general education. Social cognition activities (social perception, social judgment, social awareness, social connectedness). Begin staff lunch rotations.
12:20–12:30	Hygiene	Bathroom and hand-washing; prepare for lunch; continue staff lunch rotations.

Table 5.1, *continued*

Time	Activity	Details
12:30–1:00	Lunch	Facilitate social and communication skills as well as choice-making and functional skills; continue staff lunch rotations.
1:00–1:30	Recess	Facilitate social interactions, play skills, turn-taking, initiating conversations, and group participation.
1:30–2:00	Functional Skills	Functional reading and math skills such as community and safety signs; time and money skills; personal management; school/class jobs; and community awareness and resources.
2:00–2:30	Math/Reading Rotations	Rotations: Independent work activities; one-on-one teacher time; small group; centers (computer center, listening center, and/or sensory center).
2:30–2:45	Dismissal Activities	Closing/good-bye activity; bathroom; pack-up routine; dismissal.

can enhance comprehension and therefore may provide an additional level of clarity for an individual student.

Routines

Teachers need to implement routines to help students approach new or unfamiliar tasks by providing a familiar systematic approach or sequence to follow. Routines help students with ASD understand what is required and provide the structure needed to complete each task. Specific routines should be established and consistently reinforced. Examples of simple routines include reviewing individual schedules, engaging in independent work time activities, and associating transitions with specific music or objects. It is also helpful to have clear signals for beginning and ending segments of learning.

Work Systems

The teacher of a student with ASD should also establish work systems within the independent work area of the classroom. The work systems help a student to know what is expected during the independent work activities, how to organize the task, and how to identify what needs to be done to complete each task. Within the independent work area, the work system is the visual procedure that the student follows to initiate, engage in, and complete each task. This work system is an inherent part of the Treatment and Education of Autistic and related Communication handicapped Children (TEACCH) Structured Teaching Model for instruction (Mesibov, Shea, & Schopler, 2004). Independent tasks within this area are defined as single-organized activities with clear beginnings and ends. Individual work systems communicate what work needs to be done, how much work there is to complete, and how the student will know when he is finished. Understanding the concept of finished becomes a motivator for the student to complete the task; not understanding this concept can make working in a classroom laborious and tedious. It is also important for the skills to be meaningful and the materials to be interesting to the student in order for him to be motivated to engage in and complete the task. Once a work system has been learned, it can be applied to other environments in the student's life.

Visual Tools

Educators use visual tools to enhance the communication process and to make auditory information more clear and meaningful. They help students with ASD to attend better, know what is expected, organize information, recall information, and expand their language. There is evidence to support that students with ASD do better *visually* than auditorily, but we are often asking them to exist in an environment where the primary mode of communication (verbalization) challenges their weaker skills a majority of the time. When we present information verbally, the words are available for a brief moment. When we present information visually, it can be there for as long as the student needs it (Hodgdon, 2001).

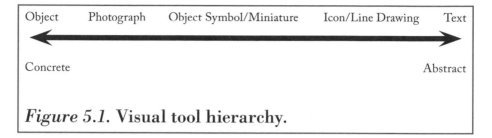

Figure 5.1. **Visual tool hierarchy.**

Teachers often present information orally, give multistep directions, and ask questions that require oral responses. These challenges therefore necessitate the use of visual tools to help students with ASD better understand, organize, and negotiate their school, home, and community environments. Visual tools need to be portable so they can go wherever the student goes. The visuals must be easily recognized, easily understood by others, and durable. Once a student becomes successful using visual supports, service providers may be tempted to remove them, but experience has shown that as children enter new environments and face new challenges, it is much easier to modify existing visual supports than to reintroduce visual supports that had been taken away!

In considering what specific visual tool to implement, teachers and family members should be thinking of the targeted purpose for its use incorporating the student's strengths and preferences. Questions to consider may include: What does the student need to understand? What would help the student participate more meaningfully in the lesson or activity? How can a visual tool help the student be more independent when beginning, participating in, and completing a task? How can a visual tool assist the student in communicating with others? Visual supports also assist with problem solving. If a teacher finds that directions need to be repeated excessively, the teacher may use a visual tool to serve as a cue for that direction or concept. If a student is asking the same question repeatedly, a visual tool may support the student's communicative efforts more efficiently and effectively.

When looking at the individual needs of students and the use of visuals, there is a developmental hierarchy from concrete to abstract that should be taken into consideration (see Figure 5.1). This visual tool hierarchy ranges from a concrete level of objects; to object symbol, miniature, or name-brand product label; to photographs; to icons/line drawings (colored, then black and white); and finally to text as the most abstract level.

Each level of the hierarchy will not be valuable unless the student can derive meaning from the visual tool that is selected. Icons, or black-lined representational images, are the most abstract use of visuals before using just words. Many students with ASD need the higher, more concrete levels of the hierarchy in order to truly comprehend the information. Students will get the greatest benefit from visuals that are most easily recognized; therefore, it is beneficial to embed a photograph of the student doing the task or working in a designated classroom area so the student can identify it/himself readily. Table 5.2 provides examples of how visual tools can be used in a classroom.

Proactive Supports for Cooperative Student Behavior

Another classroom consideration that is seminal to orderly learning and successful achievement is the implementation of positive, proactive behavior supports. It is important for educators to recognize and understand that behavior is a form of communication. Students with ASD, who by the very nature of their diagnosis have communication differences, are more likely to use behaviors to express wants and needs. Students may engage in "spicy" (or some may say, "dicey") behaviors because they have learned that these behaviors work for them. Students learn, over time, that when they exhibit a particular behavior they can obtain or avoid something. Every behavior can be described by form and function. The form is the topography of the behavior that the student uses to communicate, and the function is the reason for the behavior. Some of the more common functions of behaviors of students with ASD are: to access/obtain attention and/or a preferred object or activity (positive reinforcement); to avoid/escape something unpleasant such as avoiding a crowded cafeteria or escaping a written work task that is challenging (negative reinforcement); and to gain sensory stimulation (positive automatic reinforcement).

Table 5.2

Categories of Visual Tools That Can Be Used for a Variety of Purposes in the Classroom

Visual Schedules	Could include varying classroom and portable types of schedules as found in/on wall charts, sentence strips, folders, books, clipboards, wallets, binders, cards, students' desktops, bulletin boards, or circular key or binder rings.
Mini-Schedules	Visual forms of task analysis that separate an activity into manageable steps. Examples of routines that lend themselves well to a mini-schedule include washing hands, doing circle time activities, assembling objects, cooking, or completing bathroom routines.
Labeling and Organizing the Environment	The use of clearly identified labeling of supplies and materials, where they are kept, where students' personal belongings are housed, where students work or play, and where equipment and/or specific spaces are off-limits to students.
Cuing	A visual signal and/or a ready-reference chart intended to help students attend, stay on task, remember the current activity, remain on task, ignore distractions, teach and communicate rules, guide self-regulation, clarify verbal information, eliminate confusion, review for remembering, and/or overlearn, which results in generalization.
Social Supports	Stories, problem-solving scenarios, or pictures/icons that can be made manually or accessed in books or digital format and are used to explain social situations that may be confusing or unpredictable. Visual social supports are used to help students make sense of social/emotional experiences and understand others' perspectives.
Choice Making/ Communication	Visual supports help students to examine options, make better decisions, make choices, empower them, and ultimately give them more control. Visuals support receptive and expressive communication and word retrieval. Visuals also help students share thoughts, ideas, feelings, wants, and needs.
Adapted Materials	Accessed or created by teachers including visual supports that can simplify and clarify information so that students may learn new vocabulary; names of people; favorite toys, activities, or places; new tasks; and academic or social skills. Visuals accompanying directions help students to make sense of what is required to complete an activity, an essential skill to learn in elementary school. Using visuals to adapt existing general education curriculum is often necessary for students to be able to access the key concepts or skills.

Student behavior is functional, predictable, and changeable. When spicy behaviors appear, the educators should ask questions such as (1) Is the student tired? Hot? Hungry? (2) Is the task too boring? Too difficult? (3) Are we asking the student to make too many transitions or changes in routine? (4) Are alternative communication systems available, accessible, and effective? or (5) Are structured and motivating choices offered to increase cooperation?

As educators consider behavioral interventions, the most effective approach is prevention. The goal of educators should be to prevent disruptive behaviors from occurring in the first place, rather than waiting for them to happen. As teachers consider the individual learning profiles of their students and collect and examine data, they should review important factors discussed previously in this section of the chapter and in Chapter 3.

A classroom in which students experience the most academic, social, and behavioral success will be one in which there are clear expectations for tasks and activities, and students are explicitly taught how to participate in the activities. Additionally, the educator needs to promote interaction and participation by providing clearly defined turn-taking opportunities and by structuring activities to have a clear beginning, middle, and end. Students need to see a logical sequence of steps for tasks, activities, and routines.

The structured physical environment, predictable schedule of activities, and familiar routines all contribute to student success. As the educator learns the unique rhythms and strengths of each student, more individualized supports can be identified and anticipated. There are a variety of simple classroom and "surface" management strategies that may be helpful in preventing behaviors from ever beginning, or if they should begin, by addressing them early on before they are exacerbated. These strategies are described in Table 5.3.

Data Collection

Data-based decision making is a critical component in educating students with ASD (Handleman & Harris, 2006). Data collection of

Table 5.3

Classroom Management Strategies for Preventing/
Interrupting Problem Behaviors

Planned Ignoring	Planned ignoring (purposefully not seeing) involves the staff ignoring the behavior. This is most effective for a student who exhibits the behavior in an effort to get attention. The staff must remember to simultaneously teach an appropriate, alternative behavior that a student can use to access attention (e.g., hand raising).
Choices	Structured, limited, and purposeful choices should be given whenever possible. Examples may include: Would you like to write the answer on the board or choose a friend to write your answer for you? Which worksheet would you like to do first? This helps the student feel a sense of control and empowerment.
Schedules and To-Do Lists	Picture/icon or written agendas of the day's activities in order of occurrence (discussed in detail earlier in this chapter) can help with students who have difficulty transitioning, have trouble leaving an activity, or struggle with waiting for preferred tasks.
Communication Training	This includes teaching the student how to communicate specific needs. Students who display tantrums or other disruptive behaviors should be taught to communicate their specific needs in a more socially acceptable way. Students should be encouraged to express themselves (e.g., how to ask for a break, how to ask for help) through the use of words, alternative communication systems such as the Picture Exchange Communication System (PECS; Bondy & Frost, 1994), or gestures such as pointing. Teachers should create and teach students how to use visuals to support these communicative efforts. When a student appropriately uses a communication tool such as a "break card" or a "flash pass" to request a break, this effort must be reinforced by granting the request as soon as possible. Educators may need to provide some training or limits regarding when, how often, and where the student may go for the break.

Table 5.3, continued

Social Stories (Gray, 1993)	These are stories that are written specifically for a student to address a social need. The stories review expected, appropriate social behaviors for specific situations. Social Stories, a tool for teaching social skills to students with ASD, provide an individual with accurate information about those situations that he may find difficult or confusing. The story situation is described in detail and focuses on a few key points that include the important social cues, the events and reactions the individual might expect to occur in the situation, the actions and reactions that might be expected of him, and why people would expect those actions/reactions. The goal of the story is to increase the individual's understanding, make him more comfortable, and suggest some appropriate responses for the situation in question.
Social Autopsy (Lavoie, cited in Smith-Myles, 2004)	This is a constructive, problem-solving strategy designed to decrease the likelihood that similar social misunderstandings will reoccur. A social autopsy is facilitated by an adult as the child is guided in identifying the causes of the behavior as well as the positive and negative effects of the behavior on the student and others. The student also identifies replacement or alternative behaviors to try in the future. The student is reinforced for successful use of replacement behaviors.
Power Cards (Smith-Myles, 2004)	Power cards are visual aids that utilize a student's special interests to help him understand academic, behavioral, and social situations; routines; or the meaning of language. To teach the strategy, a script should be created that includes a brief scenario written at the student's comprehension level and includes a reference to the student's area of interest. The script should also include a discussion of how the student's hero might handle the situation, provide a brief strategy (3–5 steps) for dealing with the situation, and end with an encouraging note to the student to try the new behavior.

student responses provides helpful information to instructional teams to guide their decision making of the specific actions that are used in developing, monitoring, and evaluating IEPs and, more importantly, those to be carried out for daily instruction. Data helps teachers predict future performance of their students for placement decisions; it produces an ongoing accountability system; and it allows for dissemination of successful instructional results and corresponding interventions to share with other professionals as well as parents or guardians. It is the basis for Applied Behavioral Analysis (ABA), Response to Intervention (RtI), Curriculum-Based Assessment, and Positive Behavioral Supports (PBS).

School staff needs to analyze and interpret instructional, social, and behavioral data so they can determine the areas of need, the effectiveness of interventions, and the measurement of progress. When possible, data collection systems and procedures should be user-friendly and simple enough to use throughout the instructional program. Often, the instructional support staff, which may include the speech language pathologist, school psychologist, behavior interventionist, administrator, or other professionals, can all assist with data collection.

Successful Collaboration Among Educators, Paraeducators, and Other Adult Assistants

Another important classroom consideration is that it is essential for educators, paraeducators, and other adult assistants to work together as a team in a copacetic way to maximize student success and celebrate achievement. In order for any elementary school educational team to be effective, there are core characteristics that must be in place. These characteristics are described in Table 5.4.

Table 5.4

Core Characteristics for Successful Communication Between Classroom Staff

Clear Purpose	Classroom staff understands why the team exists and are committed to accomplishing the mission of the team. The team meets to understand each student's learning and behavioral profile and to clearly see the "big picture" of how they will work together to create the best possible educational program.
Priorities	Classroom staff members know what needs to be accomplished, who is responsible for each task/action, and the timeline for achieving team goals. The number one priority is that every classroom team member must respect the dignity and rights of every student at all times.
Roles	Classroom staff understands their roles and responsibilities for working with students, completing tasks, and demonstrating their skills and expertise. These are posted in the classroom for easy reference. All assigned duties will be carried out responsibly and in a timely manner. Each team member's schedule is posted in a visible and easily accessible manner in the classroom.
Confidentiality	Educators, paraeducators, and other adult assistants know that they have an obligation to maintain confidentiality of all information regarding students at all times unless they are collaborating with designated team members.
Decisions	Authority and decision-making responsibilities are clearly understood. All classroom staff must be supportive of classroom rules and procedures including behavioral systems.
Input and Support	Differences of opinion are dealt with openly and privately (never in front of students and/or families) and are considered important to decision making and personal growth. All team members feel comfortable brainstorming and contributing insights to facilitate finding creative solutions. Teachers willingly model and give ongoing feedback to staff following the implementation of instructional, social, and behavioral strategies.

Table 5.4, continued

Communication	Communication with families and agencies outside of the school must always go through the teacher. If a family member approaches a paraeducator or other adult assistant with questions or comments regarding the student, the parent or family member should be referred to the lead educator. Paraeducators and other adult assistants consistently provide teachers with accurate, objective information regarding the students.
Effectiveness	Classroom staff meets on a regular basis and make this time together efficient, productive, and mutually rewarding.
Success	Classroom staff celebrates even the smallest of successes and accomplishments of every student. They take time to honor and acknowledge their individual and team contributions.
Training	Ongoing opportunities are offered for reflection, feedback, and for learning new skills and ideas. The teacher is the lead in providing ongoing, daily modeling and training for paraeducators and other adult assistants. The teacher also facilitates the provision of more specialized training through outside resources.

Instructional Strategies and Supports

"It's not the wand; it's the magician."

Differentiated instruction in an elementary classroom for students with ASD (and in any classroom for that matter) is first and foremost good instruction. The proverbial saying is that "good teaching is good teaching." Teachers who instinctively understand how students learn will often say, "That strategy would be helpful to all students." With this in mind, it is important to note that the degree to which instruction is differentiated so that all students can be purposefully engaged depends on the quality of the instruction and the classroom team's ability to recognize, honor, and cultivate each student's individual abilities and interests. Together, this instructional team needs to agree and believe that each student thinks, learns, and creates in different ways, that an individual's learning is fluid and not static, and that enriching a student's learning experiences expands and deepens her potential.

The best teachers focus on what matters most about a subject and ensure that the essentials are at the core of students' experiences. The teacher needs to provide for both engagement and understanding for all learners while considering each learner's particular learning profile. If teachers want students to retain, understand, and use ideas, information, and skills they must give the students ample opportunity and practice to make sense of the new learning. Good teaching does not require that one adheres rigidly to a set theory, method, strategy, or technique. It requires that the teaching be creative, skilled, and data driven and that the instruction be designed to meet the student's unique strengths, interests, and needs. If a teacher is only concerned about covering curriculum and focusing on rigor, the results might just be "rigor mortis" (Tomlinson, 1999)!

Exemplary teaching uses a combination of evidence-based strategies and other explicit teaching methods. What needs to be solid and consistent is the actual teaching. Instructional approaches identified need to be diversified because all students with ASD are different, have varying needs and abilities, and learn in many unique ways. There is no one teaching approach or technique that will ensure success for all students with ASD. It makes more sense to select the best instructional strategies and methods to fit the student, rather than trying to make the student fit into one established instructional model of teaching. The instructional program needs to be meaningful and relevant for the student, the motivators varied, the consequences consistent, and the reinforcers constantly reviewed for their continued effectiveness.

There are a number of evidenced-based practices (e.g., Applied Behavioral Analysis [ABA] in its various forms—Discrete Trial Teaching, Pivotal Response Training, Verbal Behavior, and Errorless Learning) and other "tried and true" techniques and structures that are effective for students with ASD. Many of these were described in Chapter 3. What underlie all of these practices are the principles of behavior that are critical to good teaching. Once teachers have learned all they can in terms of the science of behavior and the various instructional practices that support the science, then they should use whatever combinations work for each student. ABA, in whatever form, is based on behavioral principles (i.e., reinforcement, prompting, shaping, fading). Because behaviorism is a science, not a teaching method, it can serve as the foundation for many different behavioral "models." No matter how much knowledge one has, it still comes down to the fact that "it's not the wand, it's the magician." The magicians (the teachers) hone their "wizardry" (craft of teaching students with ASD) when they carefully orchestrate and unfold (the planning) for the audience (the students) and "the bag of tricks" (the repertoire of approaches and strategies) in which they want them to become actively engaged and amazed (the learning experience).

Wizardry (Craft of Teaching Students With ASD)

Every magical teacher recognizes that at the core of effective teaching and learning is a student who understands the purpose of learning, is being challenged at an appropriate level, is empowered to work toward independence, and is affirmed in his ability to learn and make a contribution. These elements should be the central focus as the teacher is planning, developing supports, adjusting strategies, and assessing and reflecting on instruction. When a teacher genuinely embraces all of these essential tenets, then the magic can begin and the teacher is ready to wave the magic wand in extraordinary ways.

Orchestrates and Unfolds (The Planning)

In directing the wand for effective teaching and learning, the teacher needs to be clear in ensuring that struggling learners focus on essential understandings and skills; they don't drown in a pool of disjointed facts. Clarity increases the likelihood that a teacher can introduce the subject in a way that each student finds meaningful and interesting. Clarity also ensures that the teacher, learners, assessment, curriculum, and instruction are linked tightly in a journey likely to culminate in personal growth and individual success for each student

(Tomlinson, 1999). This means that the teacher does intentional planning; it is not incidental or random in its purpose, content, or implementation. This focus on intentional planning is responsive to each individual learner's needs guided by general principles of differentiating instruction, which include respectful tasks, flexible grouping, and ongoing assessment and adjustment.

It is important for the teacher to identify topics of study and the big ideas/core concepts (Wiggins & McTighe, 2005). Once the teacher identifies these, and begins to look at planning instruction, three important components of differentiated instruction must be considered: content, process, and product. *Content* is what students should know, understand, and be able to do as a result of learning. *Process* is a series of actions and engaging opportunities that assist students in forming connections for understanding and making sense of or "owning" the content. *Product* is how students will demonstrate and extend what they have learned, understand, and are able to do (Tomlinson, 1999). Content, process, and product can all be differentiated according to a student's readiness, interests, and/or learning profile through a range of instructional strategies. Within and among the components (content, process, and product) exist a multitude of practical teacher and student-friendly instructional strategies designed and intended to help elementary students with ASD (and all learners) to be successful.

The Bag of Tricks (The Repertoire of Instructional Strategies)

The strategies described in Table 5.5 may not belong in separate categories; these could overlap in their use and purpose. Fortunately, these instructional strategies are readily available for educators to access through Internet searches and interactive whiteboards with accompanying software. Teachers and instructional support staff need to model the process for using the learning strategies in Table 5.5, providing for guided practice, allowing for students to repeat and review the strategies while diminishing prompting and support, and moving

Table 5.5

Strategies for Presenting Information to Students With ASD

Simplify	Getting to the core concepts, facts, and skills; thinking clear, concise, and uncluttered; focusing on the concrete, specific, and literal and moving toward more abstract learning and materials; not watering down or "dumbing down" lessons; getting to the essence of the content (without all of the extra information).
Chunking	Learning more efficiently and successfully by breaking information into small, achievable increments or tasks; presenting information in a step-by-step sequential manner; linking each step or event to the previous one to show connections and see the whole.
Clarify	Recognizing and making connections (the "a ha!" moment); making the lightbulb turn on; using a variety of metacognitive (unpacking one's thinking) strategies and resources to shed light on, make explicit, and foster personal understanding; using gestures, models, and demonstrations along with verbalization as much as possible with all activities; being clear and specific about expectations for assignments and procedures and about any changes to the routine well in advance; using strategies like organization, visualization, show the answer and work backward, doing, modeling, demonstrating, talk about it, paraphrasing or rephrasing, teaching someone else, reflection, write it down, rewrite, highlight, color code, configuration, analogies, and mnemonics.
Cooperative Learning	Teaching students to work together to accomplish shared goals. Students are encouraged to ask questions, teach each other, and encourage each other to learn (Johnson & Johnson, 1982; Kagan, 1994; Slavin, 1981). Each student has a specific role and responsibility that identifies how he will contribute as an individual to the group. Cooperative learning supports the idea that diversity is something to be worked with, not negotiated around, and that the richness of the educational experience is improved for all students when they are active participants in a mutually supportive environment.
Multisensory Instruction	Incorporating multimodality learning, including visual, auditory, tactile, and kinesthetic activities to learn, reinforce, and practice skills and concepts.

toward the goal of having students begin to apply the strategies as independently as possible.

There are several key elements of cooperative learning that are important for elementary students with ASD:

- The goal structure of the group includes positive interdependence (members of the group work toward a common goal).

- There is clear individual accountability in which each person must master the material or contribute to the completion of the goal.

- The teacher teaches social skills needed for successful group work.

- The teacher monitors students' behavior in the group through observation and intervention and provides frequent feedback on how well students have worked together and what interpersonal and social skills individuals and the group needs in order to improve. Additionally, students are taught to reflect on their own behavior within the group and process with other group members.

In order to for students to work successfully and cooperatively in a group and to be contributing members, they must learn specific interpersonal skills. An excellent strategy to teach these social skills for working in a cooperative learning group is the SCORE Skills Strategy (Vernon, Schumaker, & Deshler, 1993). The five interpersonal skills included in the SCORE program are: **S**hare ideas, **C**ompliment others, **O**ffer help or encouragement, **R**ecommend changes nicely, and **E**xercise self-control. Students are also taught the acronym SEE, which stands for: how our voices **S**ound, the **E**xpression on our faces, and where we look for our **E**ye contact. These three things make up body language. Before learning to use any of the specific cooperative learning structures, students fully engage with repeated practice in learning the **SCORE** and **SEE** skills so that they are able to be successful participants in a cooperative group.

Another excellent way to develop necessary social skills for participating in cooperative learning groups is to use Role Cards (Kagan, 1994) to clarify social roles. The front of each card contains the name of the role and an accompanying visual. The back of the card contains the name of the role, a definition of the responsibilities to go with the role, and a list of sentence stems, which are scripted cues for things to say when participating in the group using that assigned role.

In order to promoting enduring understanding and learning of key facts, concepts, and essential skills, it is necessary to practice repeatedly and review learned skills and concepts in a variety of ways. Staff should reinforce all efforts and attempts so that learning can be generalized and utilized in a variety of settings.

The repertoire of instructional strategies discussed above needs to be incorporated into planning for instruction, developing curriculum, and setting up a positive, supportive classroom. Universal Design for Learning (UDL) is a learning philosophy that captures much of what has been described as "universally" good instruction in a differentiated classroom. The philosophy, embracing many of the same tenets described by Tomlinson (1999), grew out of the architectural model of designing accessibility for all. UDL is a flexible approach to curriculum and instruction that offers access for all learners and equitable opportunities to engage in successful learning (Rose & Meyer, 2006). Basic premises of UDL include the following: one size does not fit all, but rather involves alternatives and options for everyone; differentiated instruction is not an add-on, but rather a thoughtful design from the beginning stages of planning; and, finally, good differentiation allows all students to focus on the same concept or enduring understanding, entering at different points, pacing, and/or levels of complexity. UDL incorporates brain research that has found that students need to see patterns and connections and that if they have no way to make sense of massive amounts of information that is coming at them, then they tend to get confused. It just becomes traipsing over trivia (Rose, Hasselbring, Stahl, & Zabala, 2009; Rose & Meyer, 2006; Wiggins & McTighe, 1998)

UDL expects that a teacher will address the challenge of finding meaningful ways to connect required curriculum to students' lives. To accomplish this goal of making connections, it is important for the teacher to assess and access students' prior knowledge and interests to develop connections to the essential understandings related to the learning at hand. Teachers need to envision and build student learning experiences based on thematic or topical "big picture" ideas and organizing concepts that also pertain to the previous experiences and lives of students. Methods used to delve into the curriculum need to include use of technology, multiple modalities, and diverse learning preferences. The curriculum and instruction should enable all students to become more successful and independent as learners, confident individuals, and ultimately responsible citizens. The UDL framework affirms and reinforces the best ideas and practices of educators working in the field of differentiation for many decades.

Regardless of what the learning model/design chosen for use is, in differentiating instruction for students with ASD and for all students, the hidden truth is that it is the teacher who is the wizard and possesses the power to make learning magical. The wizardry comes from the sincere, empathetic belief:

- that all students can participate and be successful learners;

- that the myriad tricks found in the form of strategies teach, reinforce, and enhance the student's school experience; and

- that powerful, passionate teaching results in student learning translated to applicability and relevance throughout life.

The "wand" (teaching methodology) is only as effective and powerful as the wise teacher, a formidable force, who uses it to instill a magical energy into the classroom and make meaningful and memorable connections for and with each student and family members to use in the world outside the classroom.

Curriculum Content Considerations

In opening the door to learning opportunities for elementary students with ASD, the teacher and staff need to take a careful, focused look at the many facets of curriculum and instruction in order to be able to meet school or district standards and expectations, while at the same time meeting the unique and diverse needs of the entire class and honoring and incorporating the strengths and interests of each student. Separating curriculum and instruction is akin to distinguishing the chicken and the egg analogy. They are vital, integrated elements that allow for students to be successful learners. Finding the right keys to maximize achievement for each student requires prioritizing, balancing, and orchestrating those curricular areas that open the door to the comprehensive instructional program. Essential areas are discussed below.

Accessing Standards and the General Education Curriculum

The 1997 reauthorization of the Individuals with Disabilities Education Act (IDEA) called for providing the greatest possible access to the general education curriculum as a means for improving educational achievement for students with disabilities. Universal Design for Learning (UDL), discussed in the Instructional Strategies and Supports section, is one practice that shows promise for increasing access to the standards-based general education curriculum for students with ASD. Differentiation is achieved through the development and effective use of curricular activities and materials that provide alternatives for students with differing abilities.

In a differentiated curriculum (Hitchcock, Meyer, Rose, Jackson, 2002),

- *Goals* provide an appropriate challenge for all students.

- *Materials* have a flexible format, supporting transformation between media and multiple representations of content to support all students' learning.

- *Methods* are flexible and diverse enough to provide appropriate learning experiences, challenges, and supports for all students.

- *Assessment* is sufficiently flexible to provide accurate ongoing information that helps teachers adjust instruction and maximize learning.

Teachers will need to incorporate this information when planning for instruction while accessing grade-level content based on externally imposed standards. Viewing curriculum from the perspective of what standards need to be taught and learned and what curricular activities and instructional materials need to be incorporated and adapted to both meet the standards and address the unique learning needs of students with ASD, involves backmapping to the student's current instructional level and identifying critical prerequisite and developmental skills, as well as reinforcing foundational concepts and content learned previously. This process is reflected in Figure 5.2.

Tapping into students' interests and fascinations. As teachers use the curriculum to plan instruction for students with ASD, it is beneficial to use the student's peak interests and fascinations whenever possible. Teachers should connect the student's interests, passions, and fascinations to major content areas and standards-based curriculum. They need to find natural places in the curriculum to tie-in interests. For example, if a student is passionate or fascinated with a specific character on television or famous person in history, the teacher might incorporate that person or character when giving directions, explaining content, or delivering the lesson. Teachers can increase participation and active engagement by having the student teach others about her area of expertise or in-depth interest. Similarly, teachers can incorporate students' interests when teaching organization, self-management, and problem solving by asking students how to connect topics to their fascination (they often know how to do this easily).

Reading and written language. Reading is literally the act of decoding print and symbols, but more importantly is about understanding what is read. Reading involves accessing prior knowledge and experiences, thinking, and constructing meaning. Many students with ASD excel at decoding or sight word recognition but demonstrate challenges with sound blending and reading comprehension. These students may be able to learn segmented sound-symbol associations but have difficulty putting the segments together to see the whole. They may be stronger whole word/sight word readers due to their visual strengths. In an effort to create a balanced reading program for these

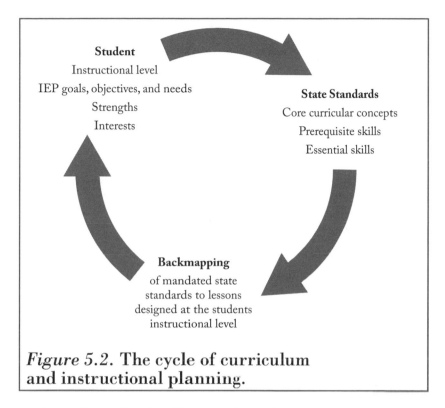

Student
Instructional level
IEP goals, objectives, and needs
Strengths
Interests

State Standards
Core curricular concepts
Prerequisite skills
Essential skills

Backmapping
of mandated state
standards to lessons
designed at the students
instructional level

Figure 5.2. The cycle of curriculum
and instructional planning.

students, the teacher should play to the student's strengths in the skills of whole word recognition and rote memory, while still working to develop phonics and phonemic awareness skills that help to unlock new words to increase vocabulary, as well as reading and written language skills.

Reading comprehension includes focusing on fundamental, literal comprehension as well as making inferences, reasoning abstractly, and generalizing. Difficulties with reading comprehension affect participation in all content areas. Teachers should develop the practice of consistently assessing a student's reading comprehension throughout daily instruction, both formally and informally. The purpose of frequent assessment is to enable the teacher to adjust and focus instruction and help students to gain clarity, use good practices, and apply the understandings to real-life experiences.

Mathematics. Students with ASD demonstrate talents, abilities, interests, and skills in the area of mathematics that could require accommodations and adaptations ranging from being highly developed to needing significant supports. Some difficulties may be related to challenges with focus/attention/concentration, organization of materials, abstract reasoning, language demands of word problems, and visual-spatial deficits. In order to address these challenges in an effective way, teachers need to plan for and provide appropriate curricular options, some of which are listed in Table 5.6

Infusing Functional Life Skills Into the Curriculum

Every student is capable of participating in the school community and community at large by learning to master the essential activities of daily living, participating in social and interpersonal activities, and integrating these into the comprehensive school program. Instructional decision making regarding the teaching and application of these skills must be individualized for each student. Decisions should reflect unique learner characteristics, chronological age, and student and family input.

Interdependence and partial participation are valid educational goals; students should not be excluded from an activity because they cannot do it independently. Additionally, meaningful instruction that reinforces activities of daily living is not limited to school settings; it takes place in the surrounding community where students can learn and practice skills in real-life settings (Ford et al., 1989).

Attention needs to be given to instructional opportunities for functional skills that naturally occur within the schedule of a typical school day. Content areas that directly prepare an elementary student to function in the real world might include skills such as personal management, general community functioning, recreation/leisure, and functional academics. Other important skills that need to be embedded within daily activities include communication, decision making, and interpersonal, social, and motor skills. Activities such as learning how to function within the school cafeteria, managing belongings at one's locker and in the classroom, playing games at recess, and

Table 5.6

Strategies for Incorporating Math Concepts Into Instructional Activities

Strategy	Use
Manipulatives	Use manipulatives designed to make learning more concrete and multisensory (e.g., calculator, number lines, manipulative clock, hundreds chart, graph paper, centimeter paper, blocks/discs for counting).
Reorganize	Provide organizational support for word problems (e.g., steps like first, second, third; color-coding; paper folding for progressive disclosure of parts/steps in the problem; sentence strips; mnemonic devices). See Instructional Strategies section for examples of the use of mnemonic devices.
Convert Problems	Convert visual problems and word problems into corresponding number sentences.
Hands-On Learning	Use walk-on number lines, walk-on clocks, and walk-on thermometers or have students take on the role of objects (they can be the hands of the clock—great for telling time, counting by 5s, or teaching elapsed time) to incorporate bodily-kinesthetic intelligence and multisensory learning.
Clarify Steps	Use color-coding, visual step-by-step models, and mnemonics to clarify, delineate, and accentuate each step of a multistep problem.
Tactile Input	Use Touch Point math to teach math facts. The strategy includes additional tactile input to help students own the information.
Visuals	Place pictures or visuals reflecting the student's interests/passions on rulers, number lines, and other mathematics activities and worksheets in order to motivate and keep the student's attention.
Passion Areas	Incorporate the student's interests/passions in word problems.
Favorites	Ask the student to consider how a favorite character/person would use a mathematics process or task to solve a problem.

performing school or classroom jobs are just a few of the functional activities that apply to all elementary students. In addition, many recreation/leisure activities can be addressed within the school and as part of extracurricular programs offered by the school and the school district (e.g., gymnastics, band, art club). It is important for teachers to consider the actual explicit teaching of functional skills and how these skills also occur naturally throughout the school day. For example, it is more meaningful to the student in charge of attendance if the teacher directly instructs her during morning routine regarding who is present and who is absent that day and then walks with her to the office to deliver the attendance cards. The student can also practice appropriate interactions with the secretary at that time. The natural application of these skills becomes a job that individual students have on a daily basis and are gradually able to perform more independently.

A significant challenge for schools is keeping a balance between teaching important and required academic skills mandated by state standards and teaching functional life skills also necessary for many students with ASD. When planning instructional units, school staff should consider the core content as well as investigate and infuse functional skills whenever possible. Life skills curriculum needs to emphasize many elements, both comprehensively and realistically, for successful personal and social adjustment. The process of establishing the functional priorities of a life skills curriculum requires the teacher to focus on core academic tasks consistent with the general education curriculum. The basis for deciding about the inclusion of a functional task is whether the individual will need the skill in question now or in the future. The selection should be governed by an objective's adaptive potential and its direct and frequent application to the individual's environment, the likelihood of its acquisition, and its impact on the reduction of dangerous or harmful behaviors. A valuable resource for focusing on naturally occurring instructional opportunities in school, at home, and in the community with special emphasis on adaptability, alternatives, and accountability is *The Syracuse Community-Referenced Curriculum Guide for Students With Moderate and Severe Disabilities* (Ford et al., 1989). If a functional curriculum is to meet the needs of a student with disabilities, then it should be developed in terms of the various ways in which the student is able to contribute and be integrated into social and community expectations. Instructional activities should be developed to assist students in maintaining social competence as successfully and productively as possible even when the curriculum is organized around traditional academic core subjects.

Directly Teaching Social Skills to Enhance Social Interaction, Social Awareness, Social Perception, Social Judgment, Social Relatedness, and Social Communication

Social interactions and social connectedness are areas in which students with ASD need the most attention through explicit instruction as well as with activities infused for ongoing practice. Students require the development and enhancement of a repertoire of acceptable everyday skills in social awareness, social perception, social judgment, and social thinking (Garcia-Winner, 2007). Developing and using these skills helps students effectively share their space with others and follow unwritten social rules assumed to be instinctively used in varying situations within a given environment. Social relatedness and reciprocity involve shared interests and experiences and appreciation of other people's thoughts, which may differ from one's own. Students with ASD often have difficulty taking other people's perspectives and empathizing with them (Baron-Cohen, 1995). This challenge, referred to as *theory of mind*, is a complex concept that includes three essential components: inferring a person's internal thoughts based upon the external behavior that he exhibits; predicting future behavior based upon one's inferences regarding internal thoughts; and modifying/ adjusting one's own behavior, based upon the judgments made. This impairment prevents students from dealing with ambiguities and nuances, causing them to prefer a concrete, black-and-white perspective. They also have difficulty with critical thinking skills involved in making inferences and predictions, both academic and social.

Communication issues for students with ASD that affect social connectedness may include pragmatic, semantic, and structural language difficulties. Often a student's pragmatic language (use of language for social purposes) interferes with the natural flow of reciprocity that occurs during conversations with people. Instead, students with ASD may talk *at* people, relaying factual information or phrases and lines memorized from TV shows and movies, without responding to what the listener is saying or doing, or not responding at all. Semantic language (understanding the meaning of words as well as shades of meaning and the multiple interpretations) often affects the student's ability to process abstract words, figurative language, slang, sarcasm, humor, and metaphors. *Structural language* (use of grammar and syntax) affects the student's ability to manipulate words within sentences and understand sentence structure that is grammatically correct (Baker, 2001).

It is often difficult for students with ASD to perceive and understand verbal and nonverbal emotional expressions. This causes further difficulties in perspective taking and subsequently leads to notable challenges when engaging in social interactions (Hobson, 1996). Most social skills and participation in any type of group (social or academic) require the ability to understand and internally take on another person's perspective. Common social skills such as greeting someone when you see them, taking turns, knowing when to stop talking, responding to others' initiations, knowing how to compromise, helping others, and/or sharing all involve taking another person's perspective. For many students with ASD, these skills must be explicitly taught. Teaching these social skills begins with recognition and a need to focus on what the student already possesses as strengths and gifts. As with all good teaching, the role of the teacher should be to use what capabilities and talents the student has and to build and expand on these.

Using the Strengths of Students With ASD to Support Socialization

Helping students with ASD to learn the multitude of strategies necessary for social connectedness and movement toward a more intact theory of mind necessitates that teachers, related-service providers, and other support staff become the "first responders" or catalysts who teach students with ASD to be aware of and to capitalize on their strengths. These strengths include the following:

- Using unique insights to find novel connections among multidisciplinary facts and ideas that allow them to create new and meaningful observations and ideas that others might not see.

- Applying independent thinking to consider unpopular or unusual possibilities that can generate new options and opportunities to pave the way for others.

- Holding firm to individual beliefs and principles rather than being swayed by social convention, others' opinions, social pressure, or fears; unique ideas can thrive, even if others disagree.

- Attending to important minutiae, which allows critical details not to be overlooked or forgotten when solving complex problems.

- Possessing multidimensional thinking, which allows the student to envision a unique perspective when designing and creating projects and solutions.

- Speaking the truth when others "conveniently" ignore what is vital to the success of a project or endeavor.

Students with ASD who do not innately and/or intuitively understand the unstated rules in social situations are often unaware of the expectations and ostracized or chastised for this lack of understanding. In their book *The Hidden Curriculum*, Smith-Myles, Trautman, and Schelvan (2004) addressed the idea of a set of unwritten rules that no one has been directly taught but that everyone is expected to know. In addition to the unwritten rules, they offer practical solutions for helping to understand and survive in this world of unwritten rules. Violations of these rules can make an individual an outcast. Some of the valuable, practical *Hidden Curriculum* topics for which there are unwritten rules include: teachers' expectations; teacher-pleasing behaviors; teacher likes and dislikes; students with whom to interact and avoid; social behaviors that attract positive or negative attention;

safe and unsafe places in the school; and "reading the teacher" and her tone/intent (e.g., when the teacher is serious or joking, when the teacher is upset).

Another important social curriculum to consider is Michelle Garcia-Winner's (1994) I-LAUGH Model. I-LAUGH is an acronym representing the many different concepts students with ASD need to consider and respond to in order to relate to those around them, interpret social information in academic and social settings (e.g., reading comprehension, in any group), and express themselves orally and in writing. These Social Thinking concepts capture and describe processes that require social interpretation and related social expression and they need to be explicitly taught and reinforced for students with ASD.

IEP Goals and Objectives: Addressing Social and Social Communication Needs

The importance of including specific social and social communication goals in the student's Individualized Education Program (IEP) is critical. Given the academic demands of the elementary school curriculum, this is often overlooked or not thoroughly addressed. Students with ASD not only need to have specific social goals included in their IEP, but specific strategies for addressing these goals throughout the curriculum should be discussed. Table 5.7 describes specific skills related to social communication, friendships, self-regulation, empathy, and conflict resolution that might be helpful to include on an IEP for elementary students with ASD.

Executive Function

Executive function is important because it affects every major aspect of learning and has implications in every content area. Executive function deficits for students with ASD can cause distractibility, impulsivity, inflexibility/rigidity, and difficulties with transitions.

These challenges create difficulties in higher order activities such as problem solving and mental planning, organizational skills, self-

Table 5.7

Sample Social Skills and Social Communication Skills Goals

Conversation Skills	Maintaining appropriate physical distance from others (personal space); being aware of tone of voice (volume, pace); greeting others; knowing when and how to interrupt; staying on topic; starting, joining, and maintaining a conversation; asking a question when not clear or not understanding what is meant; shifting topics; and getting to know someone new (Baker, 2001).
Cooperative Play Skills	Initiating, joining, and ending a play activity; playing a game and dealing with losing and winning; and taking turns, sharing, and compromising (Baker, 2001).
Friendship Management	Informal versus formal behaviors (when and with whom to be casual or familiar); getting attention in positive ways; understanding facts versus opinions; not being the "rule police"; keeping secrets and knowing when to tell them; and sharing friends. Teach students simple rules for how to join others at play (Frankel, 1996).
Self-Regulation	Recognizing feelings; remaining calm; problem solving; understanding and dealing with anger; dealing with making a mistake; trying something new; and persevering when work seems difficult. Teach students concrete alternatives for specific feelings (e.g., I feel scared so I could tell my teacher; I feel angry so I could take a walk).
Empathy	Showing understanding and cheering up a friend.
Conflict Management	Accepting "no" for an answer; dealing with being left out; accepting criticism; giving feedback to others in a positive way; having a respectful attitude; dealing with teasing; and asserting one's self

monitoring, and application of skills. Interest in a task or activity helps to maintain attention and decrease distractibility. Teachers should not assume that because a behavior is exhibited in a relatively simple and supported environment that the student is capable of carrying out or self-monitoring that same behavior in a more complex and less protected real-world environment. The teacher also cannot assume that a student understands the need for the behavior in the natural situation. A student's significant and pervasive difficulties in planning and organization should never be mistaken for laziness or noncompliance. There are a number of effective strategies for addressing executive function challenges.

Effective Elementary School Inclusive Practices

If you don't become the ocean, you'll be seasick every day.

Leonard Cohen

"Elementary schools are essential in the development of students' feelings of self-worth, social responsibility, and belonging" (Grenot-Scheyer, Abernathy, Williamson, Jubala, & Coots, 1995, p. 320). Elementary schools should be places where those charged with teaching and modeling social and academic values convey from the beginning of a child's formal education that disability does not equal deficit; disability equals difference, and difference equals uniqueness. Each unique child desires to be valued and embraced as a student by everyone and counts on the teacher to create a warm, welcoming environment in which individual gifts and strengths contribute to being an important part of the "ocean."

Educators who embrace inclusion have a fundamental belief that each individual is an important and valued member of the school community and community at large. They believe everyone can and should participate and contribute in unique ways. In order for a school to be a successful inclusive environment, everyone in the school from the principal through the faculty and all support staff need to be part of the inclusive vision, both in creating and nurturing it. Living the belief system helps to convey the message to families that they are partners in this mission.

Successful inclusion has to be a collaborative effort and an ongoing process. It cannot be implemented when one individual is making an attempt to create an inclusive classroom without the support of the administration. The leadership team sets the climate and drives the inclusive philosophy. Additionally, fellow faculty and support staff members must wholeheartedly believe in and act on the inclusive practices.

Although specialized educational environments need to be made available to support students with ASD, schools must continue to foster a continuum of services delivery model where students' goals and objectives can be met so that they are able to achieve to their greatest potential. Advantages of being in the general education classroom for students with ASD include opportunities to:

- develop relationships with same-age peers;
- learn to be part of a group and learn from the group;
- be exposed to grade-level curriculum and classroom routines; and
- have models for social interactions, social cognition, and social behaviors of same-age peers.

Keeping these advantages in mind, it is important to continually reflect upon the purposes of the placement of the student with ASD and what best fits that student's learning, social, and behavioral profile. There needs to be a commitment to nurturing a fluid and flexible educational program so that the student is getting the most benefit out of the placement. This may mean that there is willingness to combine or blend service delivery models throughout the school day. A parent's request to an IEP team that "her child increase the hours of inclusion" for the sake of increasing hours needs to be closely considered concurrently with questions such as "What will the student be doing in the increased time that is purposeful and relevant to her learning?" and "How will this help the student to achieve her greatest potential?" In the case of some students with ASD, there may be instances during which they need skills to be introduced and practiced with a great deal of structure, repetition, and review before they are able to apply the skill in a larger group setting.

Many educators and families generally understand that the Individuals with Disabilities Education Act (IDEA) dictates that public schools implement the least restrictive environment (LRE) in educating students with special needs. Oftentimes there is a tendency for special education IEP team members to assume prematurely that a particular placement is right for a child. The challenge for each team member is to keep an open mind about placement decisions until after a student's goals, objectives, supports, and services have been agreed upon. Each member of the team should consider which placement would be most appropriate, starting with the least restrictive (most inclusive) options. Under IDEA, the IEP team is supposed to choose the placement in which the student can best achieve her individualized goals and access the general education curriculum while having the maximum contact with typically developing peers. Disability labels have been used over the years to limit students' potential rather than to assist in the determination of what students need to be successful.

Special education is *not* a place; it is a range of supports and services brought to the student through the IEP. IDEA speaks to providing students with this range of services as an example of the "letter of the law." However, what enables the student to feel welcomed and willing to take risks, as well as to be an active participant in learning, is what is embedded in the "spirit of the law," which is why creating the LRE is so challenging to implement with meaningful authenticity. The major premise of LRE is to presume competence for each individual student; unfortunately, too many people begin by looking at the student's deficits and not his strengths, which should guide the student's educational program.

This section of the chapter attempts to address the spirit of the law. That includes the specific beliefs and actions that need to occur if students with ASD are to feel welcome and valued in the school and classroom setting and to thrive in their development.

A reality is that often these positive beliefs and actions that need to be implemented are met with challenges from those whose vision is not in agreement. It is possible that the challenges, while often perceived as defeating and draining, can be reframed in a positive, energizing, creative way. If educators and families of students with ASD are provided with ongoing, specific training targeted first to the beliefs on which the training is based, and secondly to the actions that will help the students to grow and learn, they may be more willing to see that challenges can be managed and even overcome. If faculty and staff possess the openness and willingness to create an inviting classroom for all, and if they are guided in learning about (and given the time and opportunity to do so) understanding the rhythms of students with ASD, they will be more likely to embrace the notion that they are instrumental in the students' achievement. Faculty and staff need to be continually reminded and encouraged to appreciate and celebrate, with the applause of parents and administrators, the small incremental successes that these students achieve, rather than to focus on what the students still cannot do. Such changes in attitude toward people with disabilities will not come as a result of legislation, litigation, or government paving the way, but rather through daily contacts and interactions with people who have disabilities and their families (Falvey, 2007).

Effective inclusive schools for students with ASD must encompass an overall vision that reflects the hope and belief that all students can fulfill their greatest potential. Without a clear vision of what is possible, all constituent groups will be confused or disgruntled. Shaping the vision necessitates providing everyone—students and adults— with skills so that they may own and proficiently apply the learning. Without acquired skills, people feel anxious because they lack confidence and competence.

Even with a clear vision and attention to teaching and reinforcing necessary skills, not all parties will buy into the need to participate fully and interact positively in an inclusive environment. Therefore, it is often necessary that the school leader build in incentives, both intrinsic and extrinsic, in order to stave off resistance that will naturally occur because people have other priorities. It is critical that people who are resistant are given the opportunity to express their reservations and be encouraged to understand other people's perspectives. Oftentimes, it is through the give and take with people who are initially skeptical that problems are resolved and creative solutions discovered. It is this understanding of the importance of considering other people's perspectives that needs to be fostered in adults as well as in their students.

One of the incentives that principals and others can provide is resources that are deemed to be effective. Without human and material resources to implement many of the strategies needed in a well-oiled, inclusive environment and program, teachers may feel frustrated and depleted. Creatively examining existing resources, varying and combining roles people can play in supporting students and bridging socialization, and considering from a green perspective what is already available for reuse and new use are all ways to use human and material resources frugally without expending excessive additional funds.

The bottom line is that without vital, feasible, focused actions to incorporate the vision, skills, incentives, and resources, all parties involved will continually feel as if they are on a treadmill, not making sufficient progress toward helping students with ASD to be successfully included. It is necessary for the actions to be a collaborative effort so that all participants see their contribution and recognize the integral part they play in the human and cognitive development of each student.

Actions for Empowerment

> Vision without action is a daydream; action
> without vision is a nightmare.
>
> Japanese Proverb

Making a plan that incorporates all of the other factors means that every team member must be readily engaged in the action. The principal is the driving force who sets the tone and motivates and leads others to work together to build an inclusive setting for students with ASD.

It is important to keep in mind that, with all learning for all people, it is hardly ever formulaic or instantaneous. It is incremental, with detours, unexpected delays, and advances. Students and educators need to be positively reinforced for effort, perseverance, and successes.

As discussed earlier in this section regarding the vision aspect of an inclusive environment, it is important that administrators, faculty, staff, and families "stop and smell the roses" to celebrate the successes and progress of each student as a way of recognizing achievement. Achievement should be measured in various ways, both formatively and summatively, as well as formally and informally. Teachers need to use their observational skills and instincts to see how a student approaches a task and what strengths or modalities are being used to complete the task. Formative assessments are an integral part of daily instruction; the teacher and support staff should be continually making instructional decisions based on how the student responds to the activity and learning experience at hand.

Concurrently, it is necessary to examine quantitative and qualitative data as a way of determining next steps and identifying how far to "raise the bar" to achieving those steps in order to move students steadily along for challenging yet attainable incremental learning. The letter of the law requires that progress is reported on each individual student at least on a quarterly basis; however, the spirit of the law would suggest that making educational decisions is a constant and continual part of good instruction and includes a spirit of creative solution-finding and taking action, as soon as it is determined to be needed, not waiting for the quarterly report to do so. Families need to be active partners in this decision making to the extent to which they are able to be involved.

Considerations that the school and family might begin to see or should ask themselves to help them to determine if the student's placement is an appropriate one could include the following: if the student has the ability to generalize academic and social skills to other settings and situations; if there is a reduction of the frequency and the amount of adult assistance and an increase in peer assistance when assistance is needed; if the student is interacting more comfortably and naturally with peers; if the student is making progress toward meeting IEP goals and objectives and is learning at a rate commensurate with abilities; if the student is actively engaged in learning by using her strengths and capabilities; if the student's behaviors show positive response to the interventions put in place; if the student is able to negotiate unanticipated changes; and if the student is responsive to the teacher's gentle, respectful insistence that she try new experiences or interests.

What is clear is that the assessment of the student's progress is as much about the student's response to the teacher and support staff as it is about the student's learning. A teacher who is gifted at working with, nurturing, and getting the most from the student with ASD is someone who

> respects students' individuality and humanity, and looks at how to bring joy and success into each student's life. Everyone is an individual and the pace of learning and styles of learning vary across students, regardless of whether or not they have a disability. (Falvey, 2005, p. ix)

Capturing the essence of each student with ASD in order to identify a single set of formulaic instructional considerations and practices is limiting, unrealistic, and nonpurposeful because it fails to recognize students as individuals.

Conclusion

I have come to the conclusion that I am the
decisive element in the classroom.

It is my personal approach that creates the climate.

It is my daily mood that makes the weather.

As a teacher, I possess a tremendous power to
make a child's life miserable or joyous.

I can be a tool of torture or an instrument of inspiration.

I can humiliate or humor, hurt or heal.

In all situations it is my personal response that decides
whether a crisis will be escalated or de-escalated
and a child humanized or de-humanized.

Hiam Ginott

Educators and families together create caring and supporting communities within classrooms and schools. All students need to participate in respectful age- and grade-appropriate work that is challenging, yet attainable. The teacher and staff, with intention, must understand, appreciate, and build upon each student's strengths and support an individual's uniqueness. Educators must be open and sensitive to understanding the complexities of their individual students with ASD and ways to help students thrive using their gifts and abilities while encouraging them to express differences in productive and meaningful ways. They must ask themselves how they can best support elementary-aged students with ASD for success through accessing their exceptional learning profiles, along with their interests and values. The goals for every student are maximum growth and individual success. Educators should always be aware of how and what they can learn from each distinctive student. They must believe that all students are competent and look for ways for every student to be an actively engaged participant in their classroom and a contributing, valued member of the educational community and the community at large.

References

Baker, J. B. (2001). *The social skills picture book.* Arlington, TX: Future Horizons.

Baron-Cohen, S. (1995). *Mindblindness: An essay on autism and theory of mind.* Cambridge, MA: The MIT Press.

Bondy, A. S., & Frost, L. A. (1994). The picture exchange communication system. *Focus on Autistic Behavior, 9,* 1–19.

Falvey, M. A. (2005). *Believe in my child with special needs!* Baltimore, MD: Brookes.

Falvey, M. A. (Ed.). (2007). *Inclusive and heterogeneous schooling: Assessment, curriculum and instruction.* Baltimore, MD: Brookes.

Ford, A., Schnorr, R., Meyer, L., Davern, L., Black, J., & Dempsey, P. (Eds.). (1989). *The Syracuse community-referenced curriculum guide for students with moderate and severe disabilities.* Baltimore, MD: Brookes.

Frankel, F. (1996). *Good friends are hard to find: Help your child find, make and keep friends.* Glendale, CA: Perspective.

Garcia-Winner, M. (1994). *Thinking about you thinking about me.* San Jose, CA: Think Social.

Garcia-Winner, M. (2007). *Thinking about you thinking about me* (2nd ed.). San Jose, CA: Think Social.

Gray, C. (1993). *The original social stories book.* Arlington, TX: Future Horizons.

Grenot-Scheyer, M., Abernathy, P., Williamson, D., Jubala, K., & Coots, J. (1995). Elementary curriculum and instruction. In M. Falvey (Ed.), *Inclusive and heterogeneous schooling: Assessment, curriculum, and instruction* (pp. 319–339). Baltimore, MD: Brookes.

Handleman, J. S., & Harris, S. L. (Eds.). (2006). *School-age education programs for children with autism.* Austin, TX: PRO-ED.

Hitchcock, C., Meyer, A., Rose, D. H., & Jackson, R. (2002). Providing new access to the general education curriculum. *Teaching Exceptional Children, 35*(2), 8–17.

Hobson, R. (1996). On not understanding minds. *Monographs of the Society for Research in Child Development, 61,* 153–160.

Hodgdon, L. Q. (2001). *Visual strategies for improving communication: Practical supports for school and home.* Troy, MI: Quirk Roberts.

Individuals with Disabilities Education Improvement Act, Pub. Law 108-446 (December 3, 2004).

Johnson, R. T., & Johnson, D. W. (Eds.). (1982). *Structuring cooperative learning: Lesson plans for teachers*. New Brighton, MN: Interaction Book Company.

Kagan, S. (1994). *Cooperative learning*. San Clemente, CA: Kagan Cooperative Learning.

Mesibov, G. B., Shea, V., & Schopler, E. (2004). *The TEACCH approach to autism spectrum disorders*. New York, NY: Springer.

National Research Council. (2001). *Educating children with autism*. Washington, DC: National Academy Press.

Rose, D., Hasselbring, T., Stahl, S., & Zabala, J. (2009). Assistive technology, NIMAS and UDL: From some students to all students. In D. G. Gordon (Ed.), *A policy reader in Universal Design for Learning* (pp. 133–154). Cambridge, MA: Harvard Education Press.

Rose, D., & Meyer, A. (Eds.). (2006). *A practical reader in Universal Design for Learning*. Cambridge, MA: Harvard Education Press.

Slavin, R. (1981). Synthesis of research on cooperative learning. *Educational Leadership, 38*, 655–660.

Smith-Myles, B. S., Trautman, M. L., & Schelvan, R. L. (2004). *The hidden curriculum: Practical solutions for understanding unstated rules in social situations*. Shawnee Mission, KS: Autism Asperger.

Tomlinson, C. (1999). *The differentiated classroom: Responding to the needs of all learners*. Thousand Oaks, CA: Sage.

Vernon, D. S., Schumaker, J. B., & Deshler, D. D. (1993). *The score skills: Social skills for cooperative groups*. Lawrence, KS: Edge Enterprises.

Wiggins, G., & McTighe, J. (1998). *Understanding by design*. Alexandria, VA: Association for Supervision and Curriculum Development.

Wiggins, G., & McTighe, J. (2005). *Understanding by design* (2nd ed.). Alexandria, VA: Association for Supervision and Curriculum Development.

chapter 6

The Development and Implementation of School Programs for Middle and High School Students With Autism Spectrum Disorders

Paul Livelli

Treat people as if they were what they
ought to be and you help them become
what they are capable of becoming.

Goethe

THIS chapter is designed for teachers and parents and focuses on descriptions of school programs at the middle and high school level for students who are diagnosed with autism spectrum disorders (ASD). It explores the differences in curriculum that occur after elementary school and how these changes relate to the instruction of students with ASD in the two environments. The chapter also discusses the need to introduce functionally based instruction and to accomplish these necessary adaptations when students with ASD are fully included in general education.

Middle and High School Programs for Students With ASD

The elementary years for students with ASD are typically spent developing the critical foundation skills necessary for students to achieve in the school environment. At the elementary level, it is less difficult to include students with ASD in general education classrooms because the academic demands tend to be less rigorous and the peer group tends to be developing as well, so the often different behaviors of students with ASD do not stand out as visibly as they may in later grades.

Although elementary school tends to be an environment that is center-based, where students are encouraged to explore and be creative, middle school tends to be about conformity. Children in elementary school have many friendship groups that often change on a daily basis, but as students get older these groups stabilize. In middle school, the idea of fitting in becomes more important and cliques begin to form—compared to elementary school, which is often a time when it is okay to be different.

Ironically in high school, the trend often reverses again. It seems to be acceptable to dye your hair purple, pierce many body parts, and wear clothes that express individualization. And it is often at the high school level where higher functioning students with ASD who can manage the academic requirements can once again fit in better with their peers, considering that many of their peers are trying to be different from the norm.

Middle and high school classes for students with ASD often fall into three categories: self-contained classes, classes where students are included for part of the day (partial inclusion), and environments where students are fully included.

Self-contained classes are usually classrooms within a typical school dedicated to students with disabilities. The teacher in a self-contained classroom for students with ASD is usually trained to work specifically with students on the spectrum or those with other severe disabilities. He or she provides the majority of the instruction throughout the day and may be with the same group of students for several years. Although these classes may be physically located in a comprehensive school, the students are typically limited in the amount of time they spend in the overall school environment. Often, students in such environments will come into contact with typical students during physical education, lunch, music, and other classes that are taught by the general education teacher with the support of the special education teacher and paraeducators.

The classes where students are included for part of their instructional day is becoming more popular since the advent of No Child Left Behind (NCLB, 2001) and the reauthorization of the Individuals with Disabilities Education Act (IDEA, 2004). The specific requirement of these two pieces of legislation—that all students have access to the general education curriculum—has led to schools shifting more of their population into these blended self-contained and partial inclusion environments.

The extent to which students with ASD are fully included, especially at the high school level, is rare but becoming *more* prevalent. It is *more* common to see school systems include students with ASD who are functioning on grade level or higher. These students spend limited amounts of time, usually at the beginning or end of the day, working on organizational skills. The rest of their days are often spent in the general education environment receiving instruction from the content certified teachers with the assistance of the special education staff who works particularly with students with Asperger's syndrome or high-functioning autism. For example, a special education teacher or paraeducator may take two or three students with ASD to an algebra class taught by the regular education math teacher. The special education teacher or paraeducator facilitates the learning for the students with ASD by adapting materials, explaining directions, running behavioral programs, or providing other interventions and support that help the students with ASD remain in that general education environment.

The Former Roadblocks of Success

Special education has experienced a tremendous evolution over the last 30 years. Schools have gone from excluding students with disabilities to finding ways to have these previously excluded students become a genuine part of the student body. Browder, Trela, and Jimenez (2007) noted that, in the past, students with significant cognitive disabilities have received little instruction on academic content. Now it is much more likely that students with disabilities are included in the fabric of the typical school life; however, this evolution did not take place easily (Newman, 2007).

The upper grades of general education settings are not readily compatible with the typical needs of students with ASD. Students with ASD tend to respond well to concrete, concise directions delivered from a specific person usually accompanied by a visual cue (Dahle & Gargiulo, 2004). Typical middle and high schools do not deliver instruction in this way. In their analysis of current research, Collins, Evans, Creech-Galloway, Karl, and Miller (2007) found that general education teachers tend to use whole-group instruction that is lecture based in general education settings. During typical lecture presentation, teachers may often include additional information about the subject matter being taught that might not have a direct relationship to the objective of the lecture—what actually needs to be learned by the students. Because students with ASD may have difficulty discerning which information delivered by the teacher is most important to process and understand, they may not benefit from the lecture presentation style.

Including students with ASD in the typical classroom has required a shift in the way that instruction is presented in the general education classroom. More often than not, schools are looking at the special education staff as a resource to the general education teacher. In these scenarios the general education teacher is responsible for instruction while the special education staff adapts materials for the regular classroom teacher. The special education staff also develops strategies that can be used to help students who tend to learn differently.

Fostering Peer Relationships

Although much work has been done in facilitating academic achievement in the inclusive environment (Browder, Wakeman, & Flowers, 2006), schools still have a long way to go in the area of building informal relationships between peers. The first step to facilitating genuine relationships for students with ASD and their peers may lie in how their typical peers are informed about autism, how these characteristics may impact behavior, and how students with ASD can be supported in the school setting. Cambell (2007) found that middle school students not familiar with ASD were more likely to harbor negative attitudes toward those students than their peers who were provided information about the syndrome. It seems that research would dictate that schools not only have to help students understand what a child with ASD experiences but also how these experiences affect the behavior of this population. Even with these initial steps taking place at many of this nation's schools, real social skills instruction, such as having and maintaining friendships and understanding what it means to be a student with limited social understanding, is just emerging (Boutot & Bryant, 2005).

The school careers of students with ASD have been affected by their lack of social skills, their "odd" stereotypic behaviors, and most importantly their difficulties with receptive and expressive language (Boutot & Bryant, 2005; Cafiero, 2001). Students with ASD typically have communication difficulties that impair their abilities to understand, process, and generate language (Alpert & Rogers-Warren, 1985; Boutot & Bryant, 2005; Browder et al., 2006; Cafiero, 2001; Goldstein, Schneider, & Thiemann, 2007; Prizant, Wetherby, Rubin, Laurent, & Rydell, 2006). Receiving instructions from their teacher, talking with peers, and simply following basic schedules can be a challenge for many students with ASD. Even students with Asperger's syndrome, who often have the skills to generate what seems like functional language, have difficulty understanding much of the nonverbal cues and higher level language associated with communication (Newman, 2007; Safran, 2002). The following case study provides an example of this situation.

> A consultant was called into the middle school to work with a student with higher functioning ASD who is included and functioning at about grade level. He had been having some behavioral troubles in class that seemed to be getting more intense. The consultant had been called prior to a manifestation hearing because the student had received a suspension for being extremely disrespectful to his teacher.
>
> During the interview with the student, the consultant asked the student what had happened in class.
>
> "I called my teacher an idiot," the student replied.
>
> "Really, why did you call her that?" the consultant asked.
>
> "Because she is," the student said with obvious disgust.
>
> "Well, what makes your teacher an idiot?" the consultant asked.
>
> "She doesn't even know what a test is."
>
> "She doesn't know what a test is?"
>
> "Yeah."
>
> "Well, how do you know that?" the consultant asked, to get some more meaning.
>
> "You're not going to believe what she said the other day."
>
> "Tell me," the consultant said.
>
> "She said, "Don't forget class 'Test is Tuesday.' She's an idiot. Everyone knows Tuesday is a day not a test."

This situation, which may seem laughable at first, happens frequently to students with ASD in school. It does not take long for an observer to sit in a regular education class and hear how much of the language requires more than a literal translation of the message. Unfortunately students with ASD often have difficulty understanding tone, innuendo, sarcasm, and other vital parts of a delivered message. It is important for both educators and parents to understand that concrete instructions, structured learning environments, and predictable classrooms are what help students with ASD to be successful in any school situation. These concepts become even more critical as these students get older (Newman, 2007).

At the middle school level, the academic gap between students with significant disabilities and their peers widens and increases the difficulties associated with the former group of students being included in the general curriculum (Carter, Clark, Cushing, & Kennedy, 2005; Chan et al., 2009; McDonell, Mathot-Buckner, Thorson, & Fister, 2001). This reality of both an academic and social gap makes it even more challenging to educate students with ASD with their nondisabled peers. As students get older, the challenges only mount.

Carter et al. (2005) pointed out that as students become more preoccupied with fitting in, they often become less likely to maintain or develop relationships with students with disabilities. As students become older and are dealing with their own developmental difficulties, the likelihood of their initiating interactions with students with ASD decreases. Yet these interactions are what students with ASD need to help them with deficits in their own communication skills. Social skills groups that include students without disabilities (or at least students who have good communication skills) and peer tutoring and peer mentoring programs are two ways in which schools can provide opportunities to facilitate greater social understanding for student with ASD. Even with these challenges, there continues to be a movement to have students with ASD receive instruction in the general education classroom as they progress through their school years.

Moving to the Upper Grades

Transition for students with ASD usually presents a time of apprehension and uncertainty. These fears are actually quite normal. Typically developing students will feel excitement, apprehension, curiosity, and concern as they approach the transition to middle and high school (Boutot & Bryant, 2005; Carter et al., 2005; McDonell et al., 2001). For the student with ASD, there are changes that accompany these transitions that have a greater effect on them than their peers.

The environments in middle and high schools tend to be very different than the lower grades. In many elementary schools, children spend their time with one or two teachers but as they transition to middle school, these students will begin to rotate classes, encounter different teachers and classmates, and experience different rules in the differing environments (Carter et al., 2005; McDonell et al., 2001). Not only are there changes to the physical environment that students with ASD have to negotiate, but there are significant changes in instructional delivery that also have an impact.

The elementary school, which oftentimes is center-based with smaller classes and more individualized instruction, is a place where students with ASD are usually able to perform better because of these circumstances, but this changes as students get older. Carter et al. (2005) asserted that as students progress in their educational years, classes become more difficult with more homework, where students are expected to be responsible for their own academic and behavioral performance. The challenges do not end here for the student with ASD.

Limit your organizational and communication skills, and take a walk through a middle or high school. Even what one might consider simple tasks, such as opening a locker, finding a classroom, and keeping track of assignments, can be overwhelming for a student with ASD (Carter et al., 2005). But there are strategies that staff members can employ to alleviate some of the dramatic effects these transitions will cause such as giving students with ASD lesson materials prior to the class so they can practice appropriate participation or color-coding materials so students with ASD can readily determine where to put these papers in organizational notebooks. For other transitions that will take place at the middle school level, visual schedules and reminders often help students with ASD navigate the particularly difficult times of change and unpredictability as they tap into the visual strengths that these students often have (Hart & Whalon, 2008). Another strategy to use is giving students a menu of possible actions they can take if they

Morning Schedule	Completed
Arrival at school by 8:15.	
Put books in locker.	
Get books for morning classes.	
Go to homeroom.	
Turn in homework at each class.	
Write down homework for each class.	
Have teacher initial calendar.	
Return to locker and drop off books.	
Get lunch and go to lunchroom.	

Figure 6.1. Sample morning schedule.

become overwhelmed or their stress level becomes too high such as taking a break to a predetermined area or a limited hall pass that can be used a certain amount of times without permission. Figure 6.1 provides an example of a morning schedule that is written out so that it is easily followed by a student, has a section for the student to record whether the step was completed, and is very portable.

When making the initial transition to secondary school, one suggestion by Carter et al. (2005) is to allow the student with ASD to shadow an older middle school student for a day or perhaps as long as several days before any transition takes place. In fact, asking non-disabled peers to be mentors for students on the spectrum can have significant benefits that will be discussed later in the chapter.

Reinforcement and Communication: Critical Components to School Success

An entire course could be taken on behavioral interventions for students with ASD. In fact, many professionals have spent their careers helping people work more successfully with students who exhibit challenging behaviors. This chapter will touch on a very small aspect of these practices. To keep it simple: Pay much attention to those behaviors one wants to increase and ignore or pay as little attention as possible to those behaviors one wishes to help a student minimize.

Although there are behavioral commonalities associated with children who have ASD, it is important to remember that autism is a spectrum disorder that will affect each child differently. One can make certain assumptions about how children with ASD will react to various environments and situations, but for every assumed reaction, one can easily find a student with ASD who does not fit the mold. Nevertheless, having a general understanding of positive behavioral support for children with ASD is critical if schools are going to include more of these students in the general education environment (Harrower & Dunlap, 2001).

Students with ASD respond extremely well to the reinforcement of behavior. Unfortunately, some of the behavior the school staff reinforces is behavior the staff would like to eliminate. For example, a student gets out of his seat and the teacher instructs him to sit down. The teacher's response has the potential to increase the number of times a student is out of his seat because the attention may provide reinforcement for the problem behavior. Another teacher in the same situation tells the student next to the student who is standing that he is doing a great job sitting in his seat. More often than not the standing student hears his peer get reinforcement and now sits to get positive reinforcement for being in his seat.

It is important to realize that any attention given to behavior has the potential to increase that behavior, and students with ASD often exhibit behavior that people seem to focus on. General education teachers need to be trained in basic behavioral interventions. Reinforcement is a powerful teaching tool for all students, but even more so for students with ASD. Be aware of external stimuli (e.g., teacher attention to nondangerous problematic behavior, eye-contact, teacher proximity) that have the potential to increase or decrease behavior (Jones & Block, 2006). Understanding these concepts for both teachers and parents, as well as understanding the relationship between a lack of communication system and behavior, is time well spent.

Functional Communication Training

Many times one will hear the erroneous notion that many students with ASD do not communicate. All students with ASD communicate. Some of those students with ASD who do not have words to speak have learned to communicate through their behavior because they have no functional system to get their needs met. Working with professionals (such as a speech-language pathologist or an assistive technology specialist) versed in augmentative communication systems and pragmatic communication training is a must for those students with ASD who cannot produce language vocally, as well as those students who seem to have the appropriate verbal skills but have a limited understanding of the nonverbal cues in communication. A lack of communication skills not only affects the behavior of students with ASD, but it also affects their ability to be a part of the class (Cafiero, 2001; Newman, 2007).

In their case study, Jones and Block (2006) found that the real challenge of including a middle school student with ASD in a general physical education class was not centered around the lack of motor skills exhibited by the student but rather the limited communication skills the student possessed that impacted her ability to interact with her peers. Students need to have a method of communication that is portable and in which peers and regular education staff have been trained to use. Too often, individuals have a communication system that works effectively for them, yet few people in the school building know how to use the device or the prompting required to facilitate the student with ASD using the system.

Inclusion of Students With ASD

In the past students with ASD were taught in separate classes where the curriculum focused predominantly on functional skills, but during the last 10 years, schools have seen significant value in trying to keep these students with their nondisabled peers. Grove and Fisher (1999) asserted that the movement toward inclusion of students with disabilities in the general education environment is one piece of the larger attempt to have people with disabilities included in the fabric of everyday social life. For students with ASD, understanding social structures and roles and recognition of nonverbal social cues and appropriate social behavior can be learned through imitation. In the included environment, students with ASD have many more opportunities to practice the skills they learn that will hopefully be used in an independent life. Having the inclusive process be effective takes some facilitation by school staff.

The peer group that the general education environment offers the student with ASD is invaluable. It becomes very difficult for special education teachers to practice good communication skills if the only peers available are those with significant communication difficulties themselves. Schools are becoming more sophisticated in using typical peers as role models for students with ASD.

Many schools have been able to get peers involved with students who have ASD especially in group work where many of these individuals may fade into the woodwork rather than be an active participant in the group process. It is often argued that students with ASD have more frequent interactions with peers and become more sophisticated in their social responses because they have the opportunity to practice those skills more frequently in an inclusive environment (Owen-Deschryver, Carr, Cale, & Blakeley-Smith, 2008). But even with good inclusive programs, there are still challenges. Owen-Deschryver et al. (2008) noted that there are limited quantities and qualities of social interactions in inclusive environments. Just because the student with ASD is in an included environment does not mean that the quality of the environment is good for him or her; it takes much work to make the inclusive environment beneficial. A good environment would have ample opportunities for teaching and practicing social interactions that relate both to the academic skills being learned and the appropriate social expectations.

Even the though the peer group is an asset for students with ASD, there may be perceived problems with the inclusive environment that lie specifically in what schools are able to teach this population in the general education environment. Jones and Block (2006) wrote that strategies for including a student with ASD should focus on providing a schedule for the activity to be taught, provide or reduce external stimuli, and facilitate relationships with peers. But these strategies do not solve the problem of what to teach these students in the upper levels. In their study, Browder, Wakeman, et al. (2007) found that teachers often question whether grade-level content is appropriate to teach to individuals with significant disabilities. Whether students with ASD receive the same instruction as their peers in the same environment or in a separate setting does not get to the core of what needs to be done differently in schools for these students.

Many children with ASD will show signs of increased anxiety and stress, especially in new or unpredictable situations, but school staff and caregivers can plan for these occasions. Schools and families that are more knowledgeable about sensory diets (providing sensory/vestibular input for a child prior to tasks that may provoke increased stress), that practice transition activities to allow children to master the techniques before they have to use them in the general environment, that structure the environment of the classroom so that visual supports are readily available, and that use social stories before students have to navigate new situations are going to be much more successful in working with students with ASD. Supports such as these are also helpful in the homes of these children.

The real question may be "How does the educational environment adapt its teaching to accommodate learners who may need more supports, and how do the other players in the life of a student with ASD contribute?" Carothers and Taylor (2004) suggested that schools and families must work together in order to have students with ASD transition successfully into the adult world. A follow-up question is certainly "How do schools adapt the material to be learned so that it is meaningful for students with ASD?" Answers to these two questions will be discussed later in the chapter, but let us first look at both the school and parent perspectives about inclusive education for students with ASD.

The School Perspective

Over the last few years, more attention has been paid to meeting standards in school. Teachers are under extreme pressure to make sure their students achieve while their classroom populations are changing. Conderman and Bresndahan (2008) found that teachers feel pulled in many directions with the increasing diversity present in their classrooms as they race to cover the required curriculum. Where does this leave students with ASD?

With the reauthorization of IDEA and the passage of NCLB, students with ASD are often in new educational placements with more significant demands. Marks, Schrader, and Levine (1999) asserted that schools are seeing more parental demand to place children in the least restrictive environment and therefore are seeing a range of disabilities in general education classrooms. But even with the changes to classroom populations, there has not been a change in the requirements of the system to meet standards. One could even argue that these standards have become more stringent. Recent expectations by educational leadership are that students with significant disabilities can learn academic content that is based on grade-level standards and that this is beneficial for their futures (Browder, Wakeman, et al., 2007). Students with ASD have been greatly affected by these shifts.

The staff members often expected to make this process successful for these students are paraeducators. In many schools, the paraeducator takes on a lead role in instructing, managing the behavior of, and developing relationships for the student with a disability in the general education classroom (Marks et al., 1999). Therefore, schools will have to pay greater attention to the training of these staff members as more challenging students are introduced into the general education setting. Instead of making decisions in response to classroom events, Marks et al. (1999) suggested that paraeducators who are included in the instructional planning process will be more effective in providing adaptations and strategies for the educational benefit of the special education student.

For students with ASD who have difficulty maintaining safe behaviors in classroom, the paraeducator is critical. Many schools use the paraeducator to facilitate the inclusion process, especially for those students who exhibit challenging behaviors (Marks et al., 1999). Initially, the paraeducators may need to give much support to the student with ASD especially if he or she presents behaviors that require intervention in the general education setting, but hopefully that support will be faded over time as the student becomes more acclimated to the structure and routines of the classroom. The goal of the paraeducator should be to shift his or her focus on one student to the whole classroom (Marks et al., 1999).

Even with a strong paraeducator in the general education classroom, the true mark of a successful inclusive experience for a student with ASD will be up to the teacher in that room. When interviewing paraeducators about their experiences with the inclusive process, Marks et al. (1999) found that they attributed the success of the placement to the general education teacher. Teachers who have structured classrooms, who use visual supports to guide instruction, who have high expectations for all students, and who differentiate instruction do well with students who have ASD.

The Parent Perspective

Parents often have mixed feelings about having their child with ASD included in the general education setting. Most of the reasons that parents provide for having their child be fully included are related to social and academic benefits especially associated with communication (Boutot & Bryant, 2005; Grove & Fisher, 1999; McDonell et al., 2001). Parents of children with ASD wish for their children to fit in with their age-mates, and they realize that similar growth toward independence for their children is equally important. In their parent interviews, Grove and Fisher (1999) found that many parents talked about their children eventually needing to be part of the community that will include work and recreation, and many of these same parents believed that the inclusive process was the first step in this direction.

Parents of students with ASD are often right on target when they identify what will help their children be successful. They talk about curriculum modification, trained paraeducators, and classroom setup when they describe what makes the difference between success and failure of an included child (Grove & Fisher, 1999). One of the problems these parents often face when their children are in an inclusive setting is the lack of a point person to contact. In the self-contained setting, parents can usually communicate with one teacher to help their child get his or her needs met. However, in an inclusive program, especially at the middle and high school level where there are multiple teachers to deal with, parents can get lost. Grove and Fisher (1999) found that parents commented that there tended to be no one contact person to facilitate the inclusive process at their child's school. For students with ASD, it is important that the IEP team identify who will communicate with the general education teachers about the student and his or her behavior and academic needs; this person can become a contact for the parents as well.

The best case scenario for students at the middle and high school levels would be one in which all students benefitted from the instruction of general education teachers. Unfortunately, the best case scenario is difficult to achieve and may leave families disappointed. It is not uncommon for parents to discover that some of their expectations about their child benefiting from being present in the general education setting were wrong. Parents often find out quickly that the philosophy of inclusion sometimes has no correlation with the resources necessary to help their child be successful (Grove & Fisher, 1999). Inclusion for the student with ASD without the proper resources and support is often a less than successful experience.

Carter et al. (2005) suggested that educators can do a lot to ease concerns for parents whose children are making a transition to a new setting such as middle or high school. How schools use their paraeducators may be the answer. Marks et al. (1999) found that paraeducators often are approached by parents to get information, make educational suggestions, and facilitate class inclusion. These staff members, along with the general education teachers who are properly trained and prepared by the special education teacher, can be the instrument that allows students with ASD to reap the benefits of being present in the regular education environment.

Helping Students With ASD Organize: Use of Schedules and Pictures

One of the challenges for a student with ASD is navigating the ever-changing world. In middle and high school, this challenge becomes even more significant as students are required to frequently transition from class to class, from teacher to teacher, and sometimes from building to building. Carothers and Taylor (2004) stated that using picture schedules are critical in helping students with ASD perform tasks independently. Staff at schools can use pictures or even symbols for those students with more skills to more easily make the many transitions. Figure 6.2 is an example of a student's daily schedule using picture symbols.

Pictures and symbols can be used during instruction as well. Identification of key words supported with picture symbols can be used to support understanding when teaching students with ASD (Browder, Trela, et al., 2007). For students with ASD who often have auditory processing problems, pictures offer a visual support that students can associate with the spoken messages they are trying to process.

PERIOD	CLASS	ROOM #
1	Calendar & Schedules	223
2	Language Arts	110
3	Computer Lab	115
4, 5	Student Jobs	Community
6	Math & Science	111
7	Gym	Gym

Figure 6.2. Daily picture schedule for a middle school student with ASD.

This chapter does not outline how teachers and parents can use pictures and schedules to help students with ASD during instructional time, but there continue to be systematic programs designed to help this population of students. Research has explored how students with ASD can be taught to manage their time using picture schedules and initiate interactions with peers using a communication book (Carter et al., 2005). Browder, Trela, et al. (2007) have found the use of task analysis (i.e., breaking the task into a "recipe" that the child can follow), picture symbols, and systematic prompting to be effective during reading instruction with students who have ASD. Students with ASD learn particularly well if tasks can be broken down to smaller parts to understand and later reconstructed to apply those smaller parts to the whole. This technique works well both with organizing and instruction (McDonell et al., 2001; Newman, 2007).

Making Instruction Predictable

Students with ASD thrive on predictability in both the behavioral and academic domains. Even in delivering instruction, the more frequently teachers can make the learning predictable, the more likely students with ASD are able to learn the material. This increase in predictability does not mean that the general education teacher needs to turn her class into an individualized format. Simple modifications to the instruction take on great meaning for those on the spectrum. For example, Collins et al. (2007) found that systematic instruction of sight words embedded into the general education curriculum resulted in students with ASD learning and maintaining those words.

During large-group instruction, students with ASD can learn if the important information is made understandable. It is often necessary for the teacher to directly identify for the student with ASD that what he or she is teaching at the moment is something the student should remember. Unfortunately, without support, students with significant disabilities, including those on the autism spectrum, have difficulty determining what is meaningful in the instruction they receive

(Conderman & Bresndahan, 2008). Predictability and guidance from support staff may prove to be critical.

Social Skills: The Real Barrier

There are certainly academic challenges for students with ASD at the middle and high school levels, but the real barrier to overcome for this population is making and keeping friends. As was stated before, middle school is often a place where students learn to conform to social norms. Students without disabilities are facing their own difficulties with the transition, so there may be less inclination to befriend a peer who is obviously different. Nevertheless, staff at these two school levels can facilitate an introduction for a student with ASD that will increase his or her chances to be accepted by peers. Researchers have found that regular education students who received clear descriptive information about a student with ASD are more likely to have positive attitudes toward that peer and perceive more similarities (Cambell, 2007). There persists the notion of not revealing a diagnosis of a student with ASD to his peers so that the student will not be stigmatized, but the research tells schools and parents differently. Eventually even the most sophisticated student with ASD will call attention to himself by exhibiting behaviors related to the disability. If his peers do not understand his behavior they will begin to avoid him and make real friendships impossible. Cambell (2007) found in his study of middle school students that a student with ASD who is introducing herself to her classmates should have an accompanying explanation of the disorder so that fellow students have a deeper understanding of the descriptive behaviors. For students who do not have the communication skills to do this, their introductions and explanations may need to be facilitated by the teaching staff. Use of an augmentative communication device that can be programmed to say some facts about the child to the class is one way to start the introduction process. Pairing the student with ASD with another student who can introduce him or her to the class is another method. Asking the class to make introductions of one another using pictures is often a way to tap into the strengths of students with ASD.

Peers who are informed about ASD can actually be great assets to a student looking to strengthen his social skills. The training of peers can increase the interactions between students with ASD and their nondisabled peers (Owen-Deschryver et al., 2008). One of the significant challenges for students on the spectrum is their reluctance to initiate an interaction, but research shows that when peers model the initiating, students with ASD learn this skill (Owen-Deschryver et al., 2008). Peer-mediated interactions have been found to be effective in helping students with ASD increase their social initiations (Owen-Deschryver et al., 2008). Yet even when students with ASD have some basic social skills, their inability to understand nonverbal communication and other social norms puts them at a disadvantage, especially as they and their peers get older.

Sometimes teaching students with ASD how to understand the feelings of others can be addressed in a rote format that enables a student to be more accepted by peers without taking the inordinate amount of time necessary to help understand the feelings of others. For instance, learning what an angry face looks like on others can be achieved through discrete instruction. When a student with ASD is successful in identifying anger-related facial expressions, he can be taught, through role-play, possible responses in situations where others may be angry. Students with ASD will experience more success in their social interactions and their peers may develop more positive thoughts about the students with ASD.

Positive thoughts peers have about students with ASD enable relationships to build based on common interests, rather than being hindered by misunderstood behavior. Students who like gaming could be paired with a student with ASD who also has a strong interest in these systems. This provides an opportunity for the two students to develop a relationship around this special interest. It may also be necessary for the student with ASD to have practiced some scripted questions and responses prior to initiating the social interaction with another student so he or she can maintain the conversation (Thiemann

& Goldstein, 2004). Programming that includes peer-tutoring, best buddies, and play groups that include both persons with and without ASD are strategies to consider when addressing these issues.

Teaching Functional Skills

Browder, Wakeman, et al. (2007) asserted that the recent national attention on education has focused on strengthening academic instruction for all students. There are obvious benefits to having students with ASD receive at least some of their instruction in the general education environment, but it is important for schools not to lose the capacity to make the skills these students learn as functional as possible. Collins et al. (2007) noted that over the last 30 years the focus on the acquisition of functional skills was considered best practice for the treatment of students with ASD and other moderate to severe disabilities. General education teachers usually have questions about how to make their instruction meaningful for students who learn so differently.

There may be ways to teach target skills based on the general curriculum that students with ASD can find useful in their futures (Browder, Wakeman, et al., 2007). One area that research has identified as critical is language arts instruction. Often, as students with disabilities progress through school they still remain at emergent levels of literacy and have few skills to decode, decipher, and comprehend text (Browder, Trela, et al., 2007). But as students age into the middle and high school levels, it is often taken for granted that basic reading skills have been acquired.

General education teachers who are using grade-level material to teach literature to their students can adapt these books so that students with ASD who are not reading at their grade level can still participate in the instruction. Books and stories can be rewritten in abbreviated fashion with simpler vocabulary and picture symbols to make the text more accessible to students with disabilities (Browder, Wakeman, et al., 2007). In response to this suggestion, the general education teacher, with all of the pressure to cover the curriculum and have students achieve at the highest level, may ask where to find the time to make such adaptations to the content being covered in class.

Browder, Wakeman, et al. (2007) suggested that teachers may want to hold book summary workdays so that the time spent adapting books and making materials can be reduced as resources are shared across the staff. With coordination, teachers can learn to share materials with other teachers so that the tasks are spread across more staff members. Also, these assignments can be assumed by a well-trained paraeducator. Parents may also be able to help, as they have been adapting materials for years for their children, and this information may be useful to classroom staff.

There are educators who believe the challenges of having students with ASD are too great and often affect the education of both the general education students as well as the students with ASD. Some educators believe that including students with significant disabilities in the general education setting is not compatible with the greater goal of having students included in the adult community (Browder, Wakeman, et al., 2007). But the general education setting offers something that students with ASD rarely encounter in the self-contained environment. Students with ASD usually have difficulty generalizing learned skills to new settings or around new people (Owen-Deschryver et al., 2008). The general education environment offers ample opportunities to experience novel tasks and settings while encountering new faces. These opportunities provide students with ASD the ability to practice newly acquired skills.

In an environment where attention is paid specifically to academic progress, it is still important for schools to keep the focus as functional as possible. In the middle school years, Carothers and Taylor (2004) asserted that students may focus on selecting appropriate clothing to wear, counting money and making change, eating out, and organizing their room at home, while in high school the focus could switch to purchasing and maintaining clothes, budgeting, preparing food, and navigating community support systems. In order to teach skills in context for students with ASD, educators need to use as many real-life materials as possible (Browder, Wakeman, et al., 2007). Just because students with ASD are in an inclusive environment does not mean schools should lose the focus of teaching practical skills within the curriculum. The objectives of the daily living skills taught to students with ASD should change as the students progress in age with a particular emphasis on generalization as the students get older (Carothers & Taylor, 2004). It is important to remember that many students with ASD do well with established routines but are often unable to perform acquired skills in unpredictable community settings.

Programs at the middle school level for students with ASD should begin to deliver instruction that focuses the skills these students will need to be independent now and later in life, such as finding the right bathroom, ordering food at restaurants, using and taking care of money, and crossing streets. Also, being able to access community resources such as libraries, grocery stores, department stores, movie theaters, doctors, and the post office will be important for their future functioning in society. The importance of having instruction that varies slightly helps teach students with ASD to be able to generalize skills from place to place and from people to people. If teachers look closely at the general education curriculum and work collaboratively with special education staff, then this all can be accomplished.

Conclusion

Research is still needed on the overall impact of academic achievement for people with ASD and on how teachers maintain a balance between these and functional skills (Browder, Wakeman, et al., 2007). Few can deny the importance of students with ASD having access to the academic, social, and behavioral skills taught in middle and high school. There are differences in curriculum that occur as students move to the middle and the high school levels, and these differences will certainly affect the instruction of students with ASD in these environments. But even with the change in environment and expectations, it is still possible for schools to have functionally based instruction where students with ASD can continue to be part of the general education setting while having their needs met.

References

Alpert, C. L., & Rogers-Warren, A. K. (1985). Communication in autistic persons: Characteristics and interventions. In S. F. Warren & A. K. Rogers-Warren (Eds.), *Teaching functional language* (pp. 123–155). Austin, TX: PRO-ED.

Boutot, A., & Bryant D. P. (2005). Social integration of students with autism in inclusive settings. *Education and Training in Developmental Disabilities, 40*(1), 14–23.

Browder, D. M., Trela, K., & Jimenez, B. (2007). Training teachers to follow a task analysis to engage middle school students with moderate to severe disabilities in grade-appropriate literature. *Focus on Autism and Other Developmental Disabilities, 22*, 206–219.

Browder, D., Wakeman, S., & Flowers, C. (2006). Assessment of progress in the general curriculum for students with disabilities. *Theory Into Practice, 45*, 249–259.

Browder, D. M., Wakeman, S. Y., Flowers, C., Rickelman, R. J., Pugalee, D., & Kavonan, M. (2007). Creating access to the general curriculum with links to grade-level content for students with significant disabilities: An explication of the concept. *The Journal of Special Education, 41*, 2–16.

Cafiero, J. M. (2001). The effect of augmentative communication intervention on the communication, behavior, and academic program of an adolescent with autism. *Focus on Autism and Other Developmental Disabilities, 16*, 179–194.

Cambell, J. M. (2007). Middle school students' response to the self-introduction of a student with autism: Effects of perceived similarity, prior awareness, and educational message. *Remedial Special Education, 28*, 163–173.

Carothers, D. E., & Taylor R. L. (2004). How teachers and parents can work together to teach daily living skills to children with autism. *Focus on Autism and Other Developmental Disabilities, 19*, 102–104.

Carter, E. W., Clark, N. M., Cushing, L. S., & Kennedy, C. H. (2005). Moving from elementary to middle school: Supporting a smooth transition for students with severe disabilities. *Teaching Exceptional Children, 37*(3), 8–14.

Chan, J., Lang, R., Rispoli, M., O'Reilly, M., Sigafoos, J., & Cole, H. (2009). Use of peer-mediated interventions in the treatment of autism spectrum disorders: A systematic review. *Research in Autism Spectrum Disorders, 3,* 876–889.

Collins, B. C., Evans, A., Creech-Galloway, C., Karl, J., & Miller, A. (2007). Comparison of the acquisition and maintenance of teaching functional and core content sight words in special and general education settings. *Focus on Autism and Other Developmental Disabilities, 22,* 220–233.

Conderman, G., & Bresndahan, V. (2008). Teaching BIG ideas in diverse middle school classrooms. *Kappa Delta Pi Report, 44,* 176–180.

Dahle, K., & Gargiulo, R. (2004). Understanding Asperger disorder: A primer for early childhood educators. *Early Childhood Education Journal, 32,* 199–203.

Goldstein, H., Schneider, N., & Thiemann, K. (2007). Peer-mediated social communication intervention: When clinical expertise informs treatment development and evaluation. *Topics in Language Disorders, 27,* 182–199.

Grove, K. A., & Fisher D. (1999). Entrepreneurs of meaning: Parents and the process of inclusive education. *Remedial and Special Education, 20,* 208–220.

Harrower, J., & Dunlap, G. (2001). Including children with autism in general education classrooms. *Behavior Modification, 25,* 762–784.

Hart, J. E., & Whalon, K. J. (2008). Promote academic engagement and communication of students with autism spectrum disorder in inclusive settings. *Intervention in School & Clinic, 44,* 116–120.

Individuals with Disabilities Education Improvement Act, Pub. Law 108-446 (December 3, 2004).

Jones, K. J., & Block, M. E. (2006). Including an autistic middle school child in general physical education: A case study. *Strategies, 19*(4), 13–16.

Marks, S. U., Schrader C., & Levine, M. (1999). Paraeducator experiences in inclusive settings: Helping, hovering, or holding their own? *Exceptional Children, 65,* 315–328.

McDonell, J., Mathot-Buckner, C., Thorson, N., & Fister, S. (2001). Supporting the inclusion of students with moderate to severe disabilities in junior high school general education classes: The effects of class-wide peer tutoring, multi-element curriculum and accommodations. *Education & Treatment of Children, 24,* 141–156.

Newman, L. (2007). *Secondary school experiences of students with autism.* Menlo Park, CA: SRI International. (NCSER 2007-3005) Retrieved from http://www.ies. ed.gov/ncser/pdf/20073005.pdf

No Child Left Behind Act, 20 U.S.C. §6301 (2001).

Owen-Deschryver, J. S., Carr, E. G., Cale, S. I., & Blakeley-Smith, A. (2008). Prompting social interactions between students with autism spectrum disorders and their peers in inclusive school settings. *Focus on Autism and Other Developmental Disabilities, 23,* 15–28.

Prizant, B., Wetherby, A., Rubin, E., Laurent, A., & Rydell, P. (2006). *The SCERTS™ Model. A comprehensive educational approach for children with autism spectrum disorders. Volume II: Program planning and intervention.* Baltimore, MD: Brookes.

Safran, J. (2002). Supporting students with Asperger's syndrome in general education. *Teaching Exceptional Children, 34*(5), 60–66.

Thiemann, K., & Goldstein, H. (2004). Effects of peer training and written-text cueing on social communication of school-age children with Pervasive Developmental Disorder. *Journal of Speech, Language, and Hearing Research, 47,* 126–144.

chapter 7

Working Effectively With Families of Children With Autism Spectrum Disorders:

Understanding Family Experience and Teaching Skills That Make a Difference

Mary Jane Weiss
and Nicole Pearson

> Other things may change us, but we
> start and end with the family.
>
> Anthony Brandt

FROM the initial ambiguity preceding diagnosis to the rigorous demands associated with securing treatment, having a child with an autism spectrum disorder inevitably affects each family member. The challenges of caring for a child with autism are significant and families cope very differently in the face of those challenges. Often, there is a focus on the negative impact that autism can have on parents, siblings, and family functioning, but the effects are more variable. Although many families report experiencing significant stress, many also report positive outcomes such as strengthened family unity and sibling relationships.

In this chapter, we will review some of those challenges, and we will delineate the positive and negative outcomes that are potential consequences of having a family member with autism. We will address the issues faced by parents as well as siblings and discuss strategies to assist each group. We will also highlight how the provision of specific kinds of support services may lessen the negative impact. As educators and clinicians, it is important to understand the family's experience and to understand the types of services that may ameliorate family stress.

For educators, it is important to understand the unique challenges and needs of these families when developing education plans and making decisions about support services. Approaching the situation by looking through the "family lens" provides educators the opportunity to not only better serve the child with ASD but also to develop a positive, collaborative relationship with the family. Such collaboration can ultimately make the difference in maximizing the child's school success. Perhaps more than other disabilities, this wider lens is necessary. Autism is a disability with pervasive effects, within the individual and between members of the family.

What makes for an effective educational plan for a child with ASD? Of course, it requires effective intervention stemming from an adequate and accurate assessment of the child, an appropriate instructional environment, supports that facilitate learning, and the collection of objective data to guide teaching. These elements of instruction in school, however, are not adequate to fully address the needs of the child with ASD. Autism is a 24-hour a day, 7 days a week disability. Children with autism live in families who are often seriously impacted by the disorder. In addition, children with autism generally do not transfer skills readily across environments without assistance. Behavioral difficulties at home may escalate and prevent community integration. When autism manifests in these ways, effective treatment simply cannot be restricted to academic instruction at school.

For parents, supporting the educational efforts of their child with autism requires a clear understanding of the instructional strategies and programming being implemented at school. Many of these strategies can and should be applied at home. The use of strategies such as reinforcement, prompting, and natural environment training in teaching children with autism is grounded in decades of evidence-based research. Families can benefit from their use not only to support their child's education goals but also improve their everyday lives. Every member of a family will benefit if he or she knows how to apply these strategies to help a child with autism better negotiate the daily tasks of living.

The goal of this chapter is to provide educators with a view from the family perspective that can support effective collaboration in serving the needs of these families and to inform parents of how their child's school-based instructional strategies can be incorporated into their daily lives.

The Impact of ASD on Families

The nature of autism—and its variability in symptoms and course—presents significant coping challenges to parents. It is well known that it is more difficult to cope with stressors that are long-term, intense, and ambiguous (Cohen et al., 1998; Lazarus & Folkman, 1984). From the outset of learning their child has ASD, parents must cope with a difficult reality that they may not have previously considered or encountered. At the same time, they are told that time is of the essence. They must act immediately to find effective services to address their child's significant needs. This is often a time-consuming and stressful process for parents, as such services can be hard to find and financially draining. The demands of trying to coordinate treatment services may leave parents with little time to spend with other family members, thus requiring a restructuring of family needs that can be difficult to balance.

Regardless of the child's age at diagnosis, the chronicity and intensity of autism creates a highly stressful and demanding situation for parents. This is especially true in the toddler and preschool years when a child's deficits in social reciprocity and communication become more evident, continually reminding parents of how different their parenting experiences are from those of their friends and families. These differences, combined with the unique stressors and worries that come with caring for a child with autism, can lead to feelings of isolation and aloneness for parents.

In addition, the variability associated with autism makes anticipation of outcome difficult. Parents read about cases in which the child "recovered" from autism, and they read about children who require lifetime custodial support. The range of outcomes is startling, and it is difficult to predict which children will gain the most skills and which children will struggle the most with the acquisition of skills. Parents need to expend energy securing and providing services, while not knowing what the future holds. Such ambiguity about the severity of autism and about the future needs of the child is hard to tolerate.

Variable Effects on Family Members

The effects on the family of having a child with autism are wide-ranging and impact each member differently. Research has shown that parents of children with autism often report higher stress levels than parents of typically developing children and parents of children with other disabilities or chronic illness (Hastings et al., 2005). Mothers often report the highest levels of distress (Bristol, 1984; Hastings et al., 2005), experiencing more sadness and depression compared to fathers (Marsh, 1993). Regulatory problems, common among children with autism that affect eating, sleeping, and emotional regulation, are also associated with maternal stress (Davis & Carter, 2008).

Although the pain experienced by fathers is not as well studied as that of mothers, it is no less significant. The externalizing behaviors of a child with autism can result in negative attention from others and make it difficult to be in public settings. Such behaviors are sources of stress to fathers (Davis & Carter, 2008) as their concerns typically center on their child's future and his or her acceptance in the community (Moes, Koegel, Schreibman, & Loos, 1992; Rodrique, Morgan, & Geffken, 1990).

Worry about the future is a stressor shared by both mothers and fathers. In addition, both parents generally report an awareness that their family's experiences are discrepant from those of other families they know (Marsh, 1993). As a result, these parents tend to experience more feelings of isolation (e.g., Seligman & Darling, 1997) and may have more difficulty managing circumstances that are significantly different from those of others in their lives. However, it is important to note that mothers and fathers also recognize many positive perceptions about their child with autism and the impact he or she has on themselves and their family (Hastings et al., 2005). For example, they often cite the child's entry into the family as having led all of the members of the family to understand what is important, to learn the value of sacrifice, to appreciate small gifts, to not take things for granted, and to work together to face adversity.

The impact that parenting a child with autism has on marriages is variable. Some couples report a tremendous strain, although others indicate that it has a strengthening effect (Seligman & Darling, 1997). It may be that the state of the marriage prior to the child's birth is predictive of how the marriage fares after diagnosis. Regardless, every family can benefit from knowing and utilizing coping strategies that may protect them from the negative effects of stress.

Coping Strategies for Parents

Each family situation is unique. The way to help any individual family to best cope with managing the realities associated with having a child with autism varies across families. It also may vary among members of the same family. However, research supports several key factors that appear to aid families in managing the negative effects of stress and facilitating greater coping and acceptance (e.g., Farran & Sparling, 1988; Honig & Winger, 1997; Weiss, 2002). These factors include social support, parent training, advocacy and involvement, and securing appropriate treatments and placements. A list of resources and newsletters with relevant information is included in the appendix.

Social Support

Having a child with autism can lead to feelings of isolation and loneliness, and social support can be a critical factor in ameliorating these feelings. Social support comes in many forms and in some instances, the perception of such support is as important as the support itself. For example, parents who feel they have individuals in their lives with whom they can share their feelings and experiences cope much better than those who do not report the availability of such support (Weiss, 2002; Wolf, Noh, Fishman, & Speechley, 1989). The interesting aspect of this finding is that perception of the availability of support may be more important than the actual receipt of such support. People are comforted when they can think of someone they could turn to for solace, assistance, or understanding about a particular need or point of distress. Feelings of isolation can also be reduced by knowing others who are in a similar situation and can relate to the issues that one faces on a daily basis (Farran & Sparling, 1988; Honig & Winger, 1997). The growing availability of parent support groups and resources within both the local and autism communities, as well as online, can promote feelings of connectedness, and help families develop networks that extend their social support options beyond their immediate friends and family. Families may be helped by suggestions to consider who in their support network can provide unique types of support, to build their network of supports through disability-specific groups, and to access such support groups.

Respite services are another form of social support in which outside professionals—often paraprofessionals or other trained individuals—temporarily relieve caregivers of their responsibilities in attending to their child with autism. These services can be provided either at home or at an off-site location, allowing parents to focus on other demands or just take a break, knowing that their child is having a positive and enjoyable experience with trained caregivers.

Parent training also helps individuals develop instrumental coping strategies by imparting specific skills that allow them to more confidently deal with difficult situations and provide a greater sense of control. Parent training programs equip parents with concrete skills that help them make a real-life impact in their child's life. It may enable them to teach the child a skill that he needs, or it may help them to reduce a challenging behavior that is interfering with family life. In either case, such training often increases parents' sense of self-efficacy. They may feel that they are finally able to effect change, to influence their child's behavior, and to have a positive impact in her life. They may feel in more control of their child's behavior and the entire family's experience (Stahmer & Gist, 2001).

Having a strong belief in one's own ability to control events is linked to better coping, as it reduces feelings of helplessness and leads to effective problem solving. Because communication challenges that often result in problem behaviors are an inherent reality of autism, empowering parents with the tools and skills required to effectively address them will improve the lives of every family member. Further, for parents of school-aged children, learning how to apply at home the instructional strategies being used in school can not only further their child's educational progress but also improve everyday functioning. Enlisting parents and siblings as collaborators in the educational process by extending efforts to the home environment benefits everyone, and most especially, the child with autism.

Instruction: Training Parents in Essential Skills

What are some core skills that we can teach parents that can lead to changes in their child's functioning and responsiveness?

The three most important skills to teach parents may be how to reinforce, how to prompt, and how to consistently respond to behavior. Why these skills? They cut across all areas of learning, increase parental effectiveness, and help parents become objective evaluators of skill acquisition and behavioral difficulty.

What Is Important to Teach Parents About Reinforcement?

Reinforcement builds behavior. It results in increased skills. To teach children to engage in new behaviors, we must provide reinforcement. With typically developing children, this process happens without much special effort. In general, children usually do more of the things that lead to parental praise—they find it motivating and rewarding. Children with autism are less responsive to praise than typically developing children. We therefore need to provide them with additional, extrinsic rewards. Naturally, our goal is always to work toward the use of social reinforcement alone. However, we have to start at a place that will be successful for the learner. This necessitates the use of rewards that are of interest to the child.

Motivating children requires a good understanding of what the child finds rewarding and interesting. What does he or she prefer? Sometimes, it is fairly easy to identify preferred items. At other times, the child may have a small number of items that are preferred, may be quite inconsistent about preferences, or may be overly focused on one or a few items and disinterested in everything else. Children with these characteristics are hard to motivate. For these children, it is important to identify their preferences and to expand them. This can often be done informally, by exposing children to a wide range of items that they may find interesting. Items can be made available in a free play context, and the child can be observed for signs of interest.

Signs of interest in particular items include:

- looking at the item;
- choosing the item;
- engaging with the item;
- manipulating the item;
- playing with the item for a long period of time;
- eating edibles;
- protesting when the item is removed; and
- looking for the item in the next array of rewards.

There are also procedures for systematically evaluating preferences in children with extremely restricted or inconsistent preferences. One such procedure is a preference assessment that parents can request from the educational team when the child is extremely hard to motivate.

The identification of reinforcers that will be motivating to a specific child is one part of the challenge in reinforcement. Another involves the proper use of reinforcement. When reinforcement is delivered, it must be immediate and contingent. Parents using reinforcers in systematic ways must be sure to use them as immediately as possible. The reinforcer must be delivered as close in time to the behavior as possible. Any delay increases the possibility that alternate, less appropriate behaviors will be reinforced instead. In addition, the reinforcer must be given contingent upon the target behavior. This means that the reinforcer must be delivered when it is earned. It also means that it must be withheld when the behavior is not demonstrated.

Immediacy and contingency are the hardest aspects of delivering reinforcement. In family life, it is difficult to deliver reinforcers immediately, as other matters also require ongoing attention. It is also difficult to be contingent. Parents of both typically developing and special needs children struggle to adhere to this guideline, as it often requires managing behavioral upset from the child. The good news is that when used correctly, reinforcement is very powerful. Identifying motivating items and delivering them effectively using reinforcement can improve learning outcomes in children with autism.

What Is Important to Teach Parents About Prompting?

Prompts are given to ensure the child makes the correct response. Prompts help reduce errors and frustration and speed up the process of acquiring skills (MacDuff, Krantz, & McClannahan, 2001). It is essential to use prompts with children with autism. Parents can be much more successful in teaching skills when they know how to use prompts effectively.

One of the biggest challenges for children with autism is a tendency to become dependent on prompts. Thus, knowing how and when to fade prompts is just as important as using them. Many children with autism will wait for assistance rather than respond independently. Parents must be taught the most effective ways to prompt in situations such as teaching their child new skills, helping their child to generalize a known skill, and when their child is failing to demonstrate a well-mastered skill. Parents also need to understand the wide variety of prompts available to use to facilitate responding.

For example, if a child is tending to request something with one word, and the team has decided to encourage longer sentences, the parent might first teach it by modeling the entire sentence, "I want apple juice." She may later provide just an initial verbal prompt, "I . . ." The parent may then simply provide a verbal reminder, "Use all of your words." Similarly, if a parent is trying to build independence in dressing, she may combine physical guidance with a picture activity schedule. Initially, she may pair the picture cue with full physical assistance on every step of the chain, then with some physical help on the harder aspects of the chain, and then with just a gestural cue to follow the pictures shown on the picture schedule.

Why Is It Important to Be Consistent?

Perhaps the greatest challenge in parenting is to be consistent in our expectations of and responses to our children. Such consistency makes the expectations clear and increases predictability for the child. Children with autism require an even greater degree of consistency than typically developing children. Furthermore, their behavioral characteristics make it more challenging as parents to follow through with expectations and consequences.

Communication between home and school is essential in this regard. As skills are mastered at school, it is important for parents to require their child to demonstrate them at home. Although typically developing children will naturally transfer learned skills to home, children with autism will often not spontaneously transfer skills across settings.

Naturalistic Instruction

For children with autism, limiting teaching to responsivity training is insufficient. Deficits in joint attention and communication, the hallmarks of autism, result in children who are not responsive, and who need the structure of Discrete Trial Instruction (DTI; also called Discrete Trial Teaching [DTT]) to build their consistency in responding to the requests and initiations of others. However, DTI does not increase skills that require initiation on the part of the child. If a child is exposed to DTI alone, her interactions with others may be passive. The child may simply wait for a cue that communication is appropriate. Such a child may, even when highly motivated, wait for someone to ask what he or she wants.

Such dependence on others is not ideal, and becomes much more problematic as children age. Furthermore, a child who does not initiate cannot readily navigate situations or environments without high levels of adult attention. In classrooms without a designated aide or in a family with other children, a child who does not initiate may not get his or her needs met in a timely fashion.

Many naturalistic ABA strategies focus on initiation. Incidental teaching, Pivotal Response Training, and natural environment training (Koegel, O'Dell, & Koegel, 1987; Laski, Charlop, & Schreibman, 1988; Sundberg & Partington, 1998, 1999) all emphasize initiation as a major component of intervention. Incidental teaching emphasizes teaching in contexts of high motivation. The teaching interaction begins with the child showing interest, a form of child initiation. It may be that the child points to bubbles on a shelf in the garage or tries to climb on the counter to reach a bag of pretzels. In both of these examples, the child initiates the chain by showing interest and is in a state of motivation to access these items. Alternately, it could be that the child initiates a conversation on a topic of interest, demonstrating his motivation to interact about a preferred topic. This was the initial definition of incidental teaching developed by Hart and Risley (1982), but it has since been expanded widely (Fenske, Krantz, & McClannahan, 2001; McGee, Krantz, & McClannahan, 1985, 1986).

The theme of incidental teaching is elaboration. Children are prompted to give more elaborate responses. Upon giving a more elaborate response, they are provided access to the object (or topic of conversation.) A child may point to bubbles. The parent may then prompt her to vocally request the bubbles ("say 'bubbles'"). When the child says "bubbles," he or she is given the bubbles.

Naturalistic strategies can also be used to teach skills that are not initiation contexts, but that involve responsiveness to others or appropriate play. Often, naturalistic strategies are used in the context of play or in the midst of daily routines. This makes them very easy for parents to use in the home.

When skills are taught in natural contexts, there are some advantages. Generalization occurs much more readily and without the additional effort that is sometimes needed when skills are taught more formally. Of course, teaching formally and in natural contexts are not incompatible strategies, and both can be employed either simultaneously or sequentially. For example, a parent may be working on imitation in DTI sessions by teaching the child to clap his hands and wave. However, when mowing the lawn, wiping the table, raking leaves, or brushing teeth, he may use the opportunities to generalize the skill. He may even use the instructions that have been used in DTI to facilitate the child's success, saying, "Copy me," "Do this," or "Do what I do." Even before the child has fully mastered the skill, parents may do the same thing while playing informally with the child. The parent may say, "Do this," while putting Thomas or Percy in the round house or when putting the cows and pigs in the toy barn. There is good evidence that teaching imitative skills in naturalistic ways increases generalization to novel settings and increases sociocommunicative behaviors (Ingersoll & Schreibman, 2006). Furthermore, using naturalistic instruction (alone or in combination with DTI) provides generalization benefits, potentially increasing both the efficiency of teaching and the availability of the response when it is needed.

Examples of Naturalistic Teaching at Home

There are many opportunities for naturalistic teaching at home. Every moment is a teachable moment, and many instructional opportunities are lost that could be captured with a bit more attention to those opportunities. For example, parents might work on identifying big and little while eating a snack of chocolate chip cookies, in which mini and regular cookies are available. Bath time can be used to build color identification skills (as the child requests different colored soap/ paints), body part identification skills, and washing skills.

Family life is comprised of daily routines. Each of these routines is rich with instructional opportunities. As the child prepares for bed, the parent can work on bathing, dressing, tooth brushing, and toileting. At meal time, the parent can work on setting the table, pouring, eating with utensils, responding to conversational questions, and so on. Free play situations can be used to increase requesting, turn taking, and sharing. Although such instruction lacks the intensity and specificity of school-based programming, it is extremely valuable. Parents who capture these opportunities enrich their child's educational lives, provide countless additional learning opportunities, and facilitate the generalization and expansion of skills.

A Note About Format

We have learned a great deal in the past few decades about the best ways to train parents and staff in behavioral techniques. In general, reading about how to act or what to do does not influence behavior. Hearing someone lecture about what to do is similarly ineffective. We need to watch others demonstrate the skill, and we need to practice the skill with feedback about our implementation. Parent training programs need to extend beyond didactic lecture. Parents need to see examples of how such skills should be done. They also need to practice the skill and get feedback about their performance so they can adjust their implementation (Lafasakis & Sturmey, 2007). Although this can be a challenge, it can also build confidence and ensure that things go well once they are initiated.

What Else Helps? Individual Characteristics That Help Coping

Parent training has been described as an instrumental coping strategy; it directly addresses the problems and teaches concrete strategies to address them.

Palliative coping strategies, or strategies that provide comfort, control, or a sense of meaning, can also help parents adapt to stress. Some individual characteristics may foster feelings of comfort and a sense of meaning. Individuals with these characteristics may be insulated from the negative effects of stress associated with having a family member with autism. In addition to a belief in one's ability to control events, holding philosophically comforting life views is also associated with positive adaptation (e.g., McCubbin & Patterson, 1983). For families, this might mean developing a broad perspective focusing on the positive benefits of their experiences in having a child with autism and ascribing important meaning to such experiences. Similarly, having an optimistic, "can do" attitude toward the inevitable challenges that will arise may also be a protective factor.

Becoming an active member in advocacy efforts, whether it's on behalf of one's own child or involvement in the broader autism community, offers additional opportunities for family members to feel a greater sense of control and meaning. On a personal level, family members can benefit from getting involved in their child's treatment and education programs. Increasingly, families are recognizing the benefits of pursuing early intensive behavioral intervention (EIBI) services such as Applied Behavior Analysis (ABA) intervention for their young child with autism. With much of the programming done in-home, parents can play an active role in teaching their child basic skills and extend his learning to more natural teaching environments as opportunities present themselves in the course of daily activities. Siblings and other family members can similarly support these teaching and learning efforts. Involving them may not only be helpful to the child with autism and/or to the sibling, but may also lead to a greater sense of family unity and teamwork.

Obtaining Effective Treatment

Securing appropriate treatment and school placements for a child with autism can be a highly stressful process for parents. They report, however, that once they are successful in securing such services, their stress lessens, and they feel a great sense of relief (Baker-Ericzon, Brookman-Frazee, & Stahmer, 2005). When their child enters a formal school program, parents can benefit greatly from joining as active members of their child's educational team, helping to steer the course of their child's treatment and ensuring that important goals are identified and met.

The most successful education outcomes are the result of effective collaborative efforts between school staff and parents. As those who know their child best, parents are able to provide valuable insight to teachers and support staff about their child's educational history, needs, strengths, abilities, and behaviors. In return, school staff can provide guidance about how a child's in-school programming can be implemented at home and work with parents to address their specific concerns and requests in the context of the classroom setting. Specific strategies and recommendations for how to best facilitate effective collaboration between school and home are provided later in this chapter.

Getting involved in the broader autism community also provides families with a greater sense of purpose by helping other families and individuals affected by autism. Involvement in such advocacy efforts also creates opportunities to forge new social relationships with other families who share similar experiences, leading to greater feelings of connectedness and support.

One final and important point for educators to keep in mind is that during the preschool and early elementary years, it is often not possible for clinicians to predict the trajectory of a particular child's disability. The ambiguity of the diagnosis and the confusion associated with accessing services leaves most parents confused and overwhelmed. Add to that the unknown future outcomes, which can range from a child having a lifelong dependence on others to becoming indistinguishable from peers, and everything in between. At the time when their child is embarking on the start of her formal educational journey, parents are faced with negotiating this ambiguous reality as well as an unknown future. It is a formidable task that can negatively affect even the most reasonable and cooperative parent. Being aware of these realities and associated challenges will help educators in serving the needs of these families effectively. Parents will be assisted by the provision of support services, by efforts to impart skills through parent training, by opportunities to join larger initiatives to help the autism community, and by being welcomed as members of the educational team.

Broadening the Lens: The Sibling Experience

Parents of children with autism are often also concerned about the impact autism is having on their entire family. In particular, they may worry about the siblings of the child with autism. In this section, we will review what is known about sibling experience and link it to service suggestions for families.

Siblings are often a child's first real partners in life. The sibling connection is deeply rooted in a shared history of family and life experiences and as such, siblings can be great sources of comfort and support. Although the intensity of the bond between siblings may vary based on gender and age differences, the fact is, the sibling relationship is often a lifelong one that changes and grows throughout life. In early childhood, the sibling role is a primary source of self-identification for many children, with the relationship becoming more reciprocal in middle childhood. In adolescence, the sibling bond may lessen as a greater emphasis is placed on peer influences and relationships. As siblings progress into adulthood, their bond often strengthens in new ways as they help one another cope with the inevitable realities of parental illness, care, and loss.

When a sibling has a disability, the relationship can be affected in many ways. In very early childhood, although typical siblings may not be fully aware of their sibling's disability, they may still detect parental stress, perceive inequities in the amount of attention given, and feel a sense of disruption in overall family life (Feiges & Weiss, 2004; Smith & Elder, 2010). As their awareness increases, siblings may experience adjustment difficulties. This is influenced by other factors such as gender, family size, and sibling age. It has been speculated that female siblings tend to be more greatly affected, as do those who are closer in age to the sibling with the disability. Older siblings have a tendency to adjust more easily than younger ones. Adjustment also appears to be better in larger families, perhaps because the presence of more children results in greater support amongst siblings and the increased focus on the child with a disability may be less obvious (Harris & Glasberg, 2003).

In much the same way that having a child with an ASD presents unique challenges for parents, siblings also are challenged. The inherent social and attention deficits present in children with autism can make it more difficult for siblings to establish close emotional bonds with them. This difficulty may be further exacerbated by the child with autism's potentially challenging and unpredictable behaviors, which can cause fear and avoidance in their typical siblings or make it difficult for them to relax at home or out in public. This may be especially true at earlier ages when they do not fully comprehend the meaning of the disability.

For parents, finding and maintaining an equitable balance of their attention and involvement with their other children can prove a daunting task. The extent of the child's disability and associated behavior problems may limit the spontaneity and frequency of family activities such as going on vacation, eating out, and attending social events. Intensive home-based interventions as well as other demands required of parents managing their child's treatment program may leave precious little time for other siblings.

Research examining the social, emotional, and academic adjustment outcomes of siblings of children with autism has offered varying results. Several studies (Hastings, 2003; Hastings et al., 2005; Kaminsky & Dewey, 2001) found that siblings of children with autism experienced less sibling intimacy, positive social interaction and nurturance and more difficulties with peer relationships than did siblings of children with Down syndrome or of typically developing children. Reported school outcomes for siblings of children with autism are also variable as the amount of research in this area, to date, has been quite limited. Bagenholm and Gillberg (as citied in Quintero & McIntyre, 2010) found that, although parents reported no differences in the behavior of siblings, teachers reported slightly more attention and conduct problems among siblings of children with disabilities than those of children without disabilities.

Conversely, several researchers have suggested that siblings of children with autism are well-adjusted, finding no significant differences in behavior, academic performance, or social-emotional adjustment (Pilowsky, Yirmiya, Doppelt, Gross-Tsur, & Shalev, 2004; Quintero & McIntyre, 2010). Positive outcomes, including having greater admiration for their brother or sister, feeling more nurturing and drawn to helping professions, and experiencing fewer feelings of competition, have also been reported by siblings of children with autism (Kaminsky & Dewey, 2001; Martins, 2007). It may be that individual characteristics and other family variables influence coping for these resilient siblings.

Coping Strategies for Siblings

All sibling relationships, regardless of the presence or absence of a disability, have their ups and downs. Although this variability may be greater in families that have a child with a disability due to the shift in the traditional sibling role, it can be mediated by fostering understanding, support, and clear communication among family members. Like their parents, siblings are often aware of how different their experiences are from those of others, especially their peers. Fostering a supportive environment that allows the sibling to safely express negative feelings not only helps with positive coping, but also establishes a foundation for ensuring good familial communication and problem solving.

It is important for parents to understand that what their typical child can say about autism does not always match what he knows about autism. Parents sometimes overestimate their typical child's understanding of autism, creating a gap between "telling" and "understanding" in which the sibling may be able to describe the disability without fully comprehending it. Providing siblings with developmentally appropriate information and ensuring they truly understand it helps reduce fear and misconceptions (Glasberg, 2000; Harris & Glasberg, 2003). Such explanations also set the stage for successful sibling coping as they influence how siblings perceive and interact with their brother or sister with autism and how well they are able to explain autism to their peers.

When discussing autism with young children (under age 9), parents can keep explanations brief and frame the sibling with autism's deficits in the context of having not yet learned or mastered particular skills like playing with others or communicating in ways typical of other kids. Parents should also offer reassurance (especially of safety), convey love and acceptance, and teach the sibling how to engage in successful interactions with his brother or sister through guided play and modeling.

By middle childhood (about age 9), most children are capable of assimilating more complex information about the nature of the problem (e.g., autism is a problem in the brain) and may benefit from learning how their sibling with autism is working to overcome her challenges. Depending upon the extent of the child with autism's behavioral problems, it may also be necessary to clarify the sibling's role in behavioral escalations. Such escalations can be disruptive, scary, and embarrassing for typical siblings. Providing them with clear explanations about why they're occurring can help alleviate some of the fear or frustration they might feel as a result.

Positive parental adjustment and coping also play a role in sibling adjustment. Once typical siblings are aware of the differences that exist in their family, they look to their parents and other family members for guidance (even if they don't verbalize it) and perceive their preferred manner of dealing with it. Thus, it is important for parents to remain aware of the impact their actions, behaviors, and decisions will have on their children. Siblings are also inevitably affected by the amount of energy and resources, in terms of time and money, that their parents expend on the treatment programs of their sibling with autism. Although inequities exist in all families, they are exacerbated in those with a child with autism. When typical siblings are dissatisfied with the differential parenting that results, their relationship with their sibling with autism is negatively impacted (Rivers & Stoneman, 2008). Parents can minimize the impact of these inequities by fostering distinct roles and interests for each child and making time for one-on-one interaction with each sibling. Such activities can go a long way in bringing some predictability and normalcy to an often unpredictable environment.

Enlisting typical siblings as mentors to their brother or sister with autism can be a fulfilling experience and promote feelings of self-efficacy and nurturing. By training the typical sibling on how to teach his or her sibling with autism a daily living skill or modeling how best to engage his or her brother or sister in simple toy play, parents can help the sibling bond grow. Keys to successful mentorship include making sure the sibling is aware of the child with autism's skills, interests, and preferences and starting with simple tasks that will lead to more opportunities for positive interactions and experiences. The value of typical siblings in these roles cannot be understated, as they provide children with autism the opportunity to socially engage and interact with others in a highly supportive environment. It also provides both siblings with a comprehensible and positive context, in which they can successfully interact with each other. Skills that may be focused on in sibling training include:

- how to get your brother's or sister's attention,
- how to reinforce him or her when he or she does well,
- how to help him or her when he or she can't do something, and
- how to know when to stop playing.

Support Services for Siblings

How can siblings be helped by the educational service provider for the child with autism? Many programs provide sibling support groups, in which siblings can come and learn about autism and meet other children who have siblings with autism. These groups can serve two purposes. First, they provide accurate information about the disability, to counter fears and misconceptions. Second, it reduces the isolation many siblings feel as they meet others who have similar challenges. If such support groups are not readily available within the school setting, education teams may be able to provide families with referrals to community-based sibling support groups.

Successful Collaboration Between Home and School

Education plays a central role in the lives of all children. From as early as 2 or 3 years old, a child will spend a majority of her waking hours in an academic environment. This is no different for the child with autism. It is important to recognize, however, that these children may have additional challenges and needs that can make negotiating and learning in a school environment a formidable task. Effective collaboration between home and school allows parents and educators to better support these unique needs in the child with autism and maximize the child's academic success.

Collaboration is, by definition, a partnership. For parents and educators, this partnership is defined by a shared motivation to use the resources, tools, and supports available within the educational environment to help the child achieve success. This relationship becomes even more critical for the child with autism, as it creates a foundation on which to build positive communication, problem solving, and advocacy efforts. Following are some recommendations for developing those relationships and ensuring effective home-school collaboration.

The inherent difficulties in language and communication shared by children with autism often means that parents and family members become the best windows into helping others understand their child in terms of likes and dislikes, skills and deficits, and strengths and challenges. This information should be shared with educational team members, including teachers and administrators as well as any others who may be providing the child with support services such as speech and language therapists, occupational or physical therapists, social workers, and psychologists.

Scheduling an initial meeting between all members of the child's educational team at the beginning of the school year provides an opportunity to discuss the child's Individualized Education Program (IEP) and related goals and services. It also gives the team a chance to determine how best to facilitate ongoing communication throughout the school year for discussing the child's progress.

Similarly, although parents are typically invited to meet their child's teacher a few weeks into the school year during a "back to school" night or parent-teacher conferences, those with children with autism may benefit from setting up a separate meeting with their child's classroom teacher within the first few days of the start of school. This can be helpful for several reasons. First, it kick-starts the development of those critical collaborative relationships and gives parents and teachers the opportunity to establish some important communication systems from the outset. Parents and teachers should work together to determine the best methods for regular communication about the child—whether that is daily or weekly e-mails, phone calls, or notes home.

Having a regular dialogue is important for teachers to keep parents informed of their child's progress as well as let them know of any particular programs, skills, or activities that they think should be carried forward and implemented at home. Likewise, if there is a particular system or reinforcer that is working well at home, parents should share this valuable information with teachers, as it might be something that can be utilized or replicated to motivate learning in the classroom. Consistency and continuity are hallmarks of successful instruction for children with autism, so extending teaching and learning efforts across both home and school environments are keys to achieving academic success.

For parents, regular communication with the school should include providing ongoing updates about any status changes with their child such as eating, sleeping, and medication or medical/physical health issues. Again, the use of e-mail or a home-school notebook in which parents and teachers can maintain a running dialogue about needs, concerns, or changes related to the child can support these efforts. Also, informing the educational team of any other therapies the child is engaging in outside of school is important. Educators can encourage further collaboration by inviting those other providers or therapists to be part of the educational team as they can offer valuable insight into how and what they're working on with the child. Such efforts can also assist in problem solving for particular issues or difficulties the child is experiencing by enlisting multiple informed viewpoints.

One final note about communication is that both educators and parents should create opportunities for sharing positive feedback with one another as it can strengthen collaborative efforts. Too often, the majority of home-school communication revolves around problem discussions and issues. Taking time to highlight a child's progress, both in the classroom and at home, serves as positive reinforcement of the daily efforts being made on everyone's part.

Teachers might also consider ways to involve the student's parents in the classroom, such as inviting them to spend a few hours observing instruction or encouraging them to volunteer at school functions. Using tools such as a home-school activity checklist informs parents of their child's programs and helps them to better understand their child's daily activities.

Schools can serve as a valuable support resource for parents of children with autism. Educators in the autism field often work with many outside agencies and service providers and thus become excellent sources for creating referral networks for families. Sharing information about parent and sibling support groups, advocacy organizations, professional research articles, and local respite services allow educators to help families better cope with the challenges of living with autism. The benefits of collaborative relationships between educators and families with children with autism cannot be understated in maximizing academic success. Collaboration creates opportunities for joint input in programming decisions and mutual goal setting. Ongoing communication helps ensure that the child with autism is progressing and that goals are revisited frequently and amended as necessary. Through positive, joint collaboration, school instruction can be carried over at home, data and best practices can be shared, and schools can serve as helpful support resources to families. All of these cooperative efforts ultimately contribute to the shared mutual goal of educators and parents—success for the child with autism.

Conclusion

Autism is a disorder that affects the entire family. Parents struggle to cope with the formidable challenges in accepting the diagnosis, securing services, and coping with the ambiguity of their child's course and outcome. In addition, siblings struggle with the practical and emotional consequences of having a brother or sister with autism. The unpredictability and pervasiveness of autism make it an everyday stressor for the entire family.

School personnel are essential partners for parents of children with autism. The success of the family in coping and the progress of the child are influenced by the functionality of the relationship between family and school. The needs of a child with autism exceed those of most special needs students and require significant resources. The needs of their families also exceed those of most families, and resources must also be allocated to assist them. Parent training is essential to meet the comprehensive needs of these students across settings. Training and support services to parents and siblings can increase family adjustment and improve child outcomes. Collaboration between home and school is an important element of successful education for this population of children.

References

Baker-Ericzon, M. J., Brookman-Frazee, L., & Stahmer, A. (2005). Stress levels and adaptability in parents of toddlers with and without autism spectrum disorders. *Research and Practice for Persons With Severe Disabilities, 30,* 194–204.

Bristol, M. M. (1984). Family resources and successful adaptation to autistic children. In E. Schopler & G. Mesibov (Eds.), *The effects of autism on the family* (pp. 289–310). New York, NY: Plenum.

Cohen, S., Frank, E., Doyle, W. J., Skoner, D. P., Rabin, B. S., & Gwaltuey,

J. M., Jr. (1998). Types of stressors that increase susceptibility to the common cold in healthy adults. *Health Psychology, 17,* 214–223.

Davis, N., & Carter, A. (2008). Parenting stress in mothers and fathers of toddlers with autism spectrum disorders: Associations with child characteristics. *Journal of Autism and Developmental Disorders, 38,* 1278–1291.

Farran, D. C., & Sparling, J. (1988). Coping styles in families of handicapped children. In J. J. Gallagher & P. M. Vietze (Eds.), *Families of handicapped persons* (pp. 143–156). Baltimore, MD: Brookes.

Feiges, L. S., & Weiss, M. J. (2004). *Sibling stories: Growing up with a brother or sister on the autism spectrum.* Shawnee Mission, KS: Autism Asperger.

Fenske, E. C., Krantz, P. J., & McClannahan, L. E. (2001). Incidental teaching: A not-so-discrete-trial teaching procedure. In C. Maurice, G. Green, & R. M. Foxx (Eds.), *Making a difference: Behavioral intervention for autism* (pp. 75–82). Austin, TX: PRO-ED.

Glasberg, B. A. (2000). The development of siblings' understanding of autism and related disorders. *Journal of Autism and Developmental Disorders, 30,* 143–156.

Harris, S. L., & Glasberg, B. A. (2003). *Siblings of children with autism.* Bethesda, MD: Woodbine House.

Hart, B. M., & Risley, T. R. (1982). *How to use incidental teaching for elaborating language.* Austin, TX: PRO-ED.

Hastings, R. P. (2003). Brief report: Behavioral adjustment of siblings of children with autism. *Journal of Autism and Developmental Disabilities, 33,* 99–104.

Hastings, R. P., Kovshoff, H., Ward, N. J., Espinosa, F. D., Brown, T., & Remington, B. (2005). Systems analysis of stress and positive perceptions in mothers and fathers of pre-school children with autism. *Journal of Autism and Developmental Disorders, 35,* 635–644.

Honig, A. S., & Winger, C. J. (1997). A professional support program for families of handicapped preschoolers: Decrease in maternal stress. *Journal of Primary Prevention, 17,* 285–296.

Ingersoll, B., & Schreibman, L. (2006). Teaching reciprocal imitation skills to young children with autism using a naturalistic behavioral approach:

Effects on language, pretend play, and joint attention. *Journal of Autism and Developmental Disorders, 36,* 487–505.

Kaminsky, L., & Dewey, D. (2001). Sibling relationships of children with autism. *Journal of Autism and Developmental Disorders, 31,* 399–410.

Koegel, R. L., O'Dell, M. C., & Koegel, L. K. (1987). A natural language teaching paradigm for nonverbal autistic children. *Journal of Autism and Developmental Disorders, 17,* 187–200.

Lafasakis, M., & Sturmey, P. (2007). Training parent implementation of discrete-trial teaching: Effects on generalization of parent teaching and child correct responding. *Journal of Applied Behavior Analysis, 40,* 685–689.

Laski, K. E., Charlop, M. H., & Schreibman, L. (1988). Training parents to use the natural language paradigm to increase their children's speech. *Journal of Applied Behavior Analysis, 21,* 391–400.

Lazarus, R. S., & Folkman, S. (1984). *Stress, appraisal and coping.* New York, NY: Springer.

MacDuff, G., Krantz, P., & McClannahan, L. (2001). Prompts and prompt fading strategies for people with autism. In C. Maurice, G. Green, & S. Luce (Eds.), *Making a difference* (pp. 37–50). Austin, TX: PRO-ED.

Marsh, D. T. (1993). *Families and mental retardation.* New York, NY: Praeger.

Martins, M. (2007). *Siblings of individuals with autism: Psychological functioning and the developmental tasks of young adulthood* (Unpublished doctoral dissertation). Rutgers University, New Jersey.

McCubbin, H., & Patterson, J. (1983). Family stress adaptation: A double ABCX model of family behavior. In H. I. McCubbin, M. Sussman, & J. Patterson (Eds.), *Social stress and the family: Advances and developments in family stress theory and research* (pp. 7–73). New York, NY: Haworth.

McGee, G. G., Krantz, P. J., & McClannahan, L. E. (1985). The facilitative effects of incidental teaching on preposition use by autistic children. *Journal of Applied Behavior Analysis, 18,* 17–31.

McGee, G. G., Krantz, P. J., & McClannahan, L. E. (1986). An extension of incidental teaching procedures to reading instruction for autistic children. *Journal of Applied Behavior Analysis, 19,* 147–157.

Moes, D. J., Koegel, R. L., Schreibman, L., & Loos, L. M. (1992). Stress profiles for mothers and fathers of children with autism. *Psychological Reports, 71,* 1272–1274.

Pilowsky, T., Yirmiya, N., Doppelt, O., Gross-Tsur, V., & Shalev, R. S. (2004). Social and emotional adjustment of siblings of children with autism. *Journal of Child Psychology and Psychiatry, 45,* 855–865.

Quintero, N., & McIntyre, L. L. (2010). Sibling adjustment and maternal well-being: An examination of families with and without a child with an autism spectrum disorder. *Focus on Autism and Other Developmental Disabilities, 25,* 37–46.

Rivers, J. W., & Stoneman, Z. (2008). Child temperaments, differential parenting, and the sibling relationships of children with autism spectrum disorders. *Journal of Autism and Developmental Disorders, 38,* 1740–1750.

Rodrique, J. R., Morgan, S. B., & Geffken, G. (1990). Families of autistic children: Psychosocial functioning of mothers. *Journal of Child Clinical Psychology, 19,* 371–379.

Seligman, M., & Darling, R. B. (1997). *Ordinary families, special children.* New York, NY: Guilford.

Smith, L. O., & Elder, J. H. (2010). Siblings and family environments of persons with autism spectrum disorder: A review of the literature. *Journal of Child and Adolescent Psychiatry Nursing, 23,* 189–195.

Stahmer, A. C., & Gist, K. (2001). Enhancing parent training through additional support services. *Journal of Positive Behavior Interventions, 3,* 75–82.

Sundberg, M. L., & Partington, J. W. (1998). *Teaching language to children with autism or other developmental disabilities.* Pleasant Hill, CA: Behavior Analysts.

Sundberg, M. L., & Partington, J. W. (1999). The need for both DT and NE training for children with autism. In P. M. Ghezzi, W. L. Williams, & J. E. Carr (Eds.), *Autism: Behavior analytic approaches* (pp. 139–156). Reno, NV: Context Press.

Weiss, M. J. (2002). Hardiness and social support as predictors of stress in mothers of typical children, children with autism, and children with mental retardation. *Autism, 6,* 115–130.

Wolf, L. C., Noh, S., Fishman, S. N., & Speechley, M. (1989). Psychological effects of parenting stress on parents of autistic children. *Journal of Autism and Developmental Disorders, 19*, 157–166.

Conclusion

Andrew L. Egel,
Katherine C. Holman,
and Christine Barthold

Never doubt that a small group of thoughtful
committed citizens can change the world;
indeed it is the only thing that ever has.

Margaret Mead

I T is our hope that you have found this book to
be a practical resource for information related to
the characteristics of individuals with ASD, their
unique learning needs and gifts, the importance of
a thorough assessment, and specific instructional
programming to ensure successful school experiences for students with ASD throughout their
academic career. As the editors, we have brought
together a wealth of resources from experts in the
field who know firsthand how to create effective
school programs. Each chapter was designed to
give both parents and teachers alike critical components to consider when either looking for a
classroom setting for their child or planning an

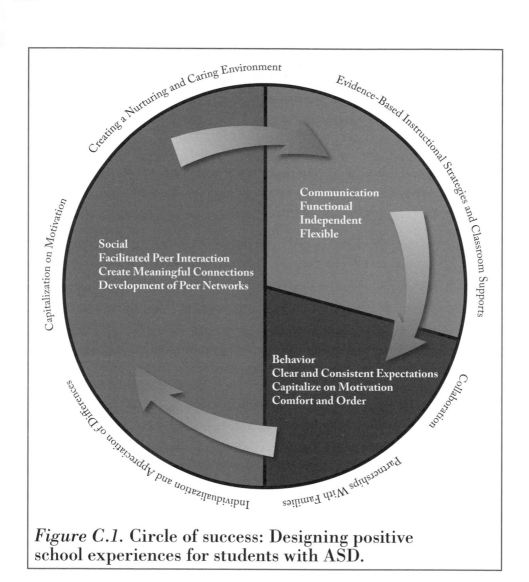

Figure C.1. Circle of success: Designing positive school experiences for students with ASD.

effective educational experience for a student with ASD. Figure C.1 summarizes the main points of the book while surrounding the three core areas of need that require direct support for students with ASD. When these elements are put into place in the academic setting, one is able to see that students with ASD can learn, engage with others, and make important contributions to the classroom and beyond.

As we return to the theme from the introduction (of our favorite friends coming over for a visit), we are reminded that beyond the curriculum and instructional strategies, school success for students with ASD begins and ends with meaningful relationships. To this end, we have interwoven the importance of developing meaningful relationships (between student and teacher, student and peer, and teacher and families) throughout the entire book, showing our agreement with the words of Antoine de Saint-Exupéry: "there is no hope or joy except in human relations." Students with ASD may be able to follow a visual picture schedule or complete an independent workstation, but if they are unable to communicate socially with another person and develop a relationship with others, we have failed to adequately address the whole child.

This is the primary deficiency in individuals with ASD. Impoverished social connections are one of the first noticeable characteristics in young children with ASD, and it is the most pervasive impairment throughout their lives. The importance of directly targeting social development and facilitating social interactions at an early age was explained in the preschool chapter, the importance of providing direct instruction on social skills and the creation of connections for individuals with ASD was highlighted in the elementary school chapter, the importance of developing peer networks and focused opportunities for supported social interactions was discussed in the middle and high school chapter, and finally, the crucial component of building relationships with families by supporting and empowering them was thoroughly described in the final chapter.

It is our hope that after reading this book, you will approach the education of a child with ASD with a positive and willing attitude. The tools for creating an effective classroom environment and assisting the individual with ASD to achieve both academic and social success have been shared in great detail, and now it is your opportunity to use this information to create meaningful relationships and have a significant impact on the life of a student with ASD.

Resources for Helping Kids With Autism

PLEASE note that this is not an exhaustive list of resources. Many local and regional resources could also be very useful and many can be found via the online directory listings provided. The information provided in this appendix is not a recommendation, referral, or endorsement of any resource, therapeutic method, or service provider by the authors or publisher. It does not replace the advice of professionals familiar with your child or student.

Resources for General Instruction Strategies

Association for Science in Autism Treatment—http://www. asatonline.org

Autism Internet Modules—http://www.autisminternet modules.org

The National Professional Development Center on Autism Spectrum Disorders—http://autismpdc.fpg.unc.edu

Real Look Autism—http://www.reallookautism.com

Rethink Autism—http://www.rethinkautism.com

Ashcroft, W., Argiro, S., & Keohane, J. (2010). *Success strategies for teaching kids with autism*. Waco, TX: Prufrock Press.

Bondy, A., & Frost, L. (2002). *A picture's worth: PECS and other visual communication strategies in autism*. Baltimore, MD: Woodbine House.

Grandin, T. (2010). *Thinking in pictures and other reports from my life with autism*. New York, NY: Vintage Books.

Hamilton, L. M. (2000). *Facing autism: Giving parents reason for hope and guidance for help*. Colorado Springs, CO: Waterbrook Press.

Harris, S., & Weiss, M. J. (2007). *Right from the start: Behavioral intervention for young children with autism*. Bethesda, MD: Woodbine House.

Kearney, A. J. (2008). *Understanding applied behavior analysis: An introduction to ABA for parents, teachers, and other professionals*. London, UK: Jessica Kingsley.

Koegel, L. K., Koegel, R. L., & Dunlap, G. (1996). *Positive behavioral support: Including young people with difficult behavior in the community*. Baltimore, MD: Brookes.

McClanahan, L. E., & Krantz, P. J. (2010). *Activity schedules for children with autism*. Bethesda, MD: Woodbine House.

Newman, B., Reeves, K. F., Reeves, S. A., & Ryan, C. S. (2003). *Behaviorspeak: A glossary of terms in applied behavior analysis*. Long Beach, NY: Dove and Orca.

Newman, B., Reinecke, D. R., & Hammond, T. (2005). *Behaviorask: Straight answers to your ABA programming questions*. Long Beach, NY: Dove and Orca.

Powers, M. D. (2000). *Children with autism: A parents' guide* (2nd ed.). Bethesda, MD: Woodbine House

Simpson, R. L., & Smith Myles, D. (2011). *Asperger syndrome and high-functioning autism: A guide for effective practice* (3rd ed.). Austin, TX: Pro-Ed.

Volkmar, F. R., & Wiesner, L. A. (2009). *A practical guide to autism: What every parent, family member, and teacher need to know.* Hoboken, NJ: John Wiley & Sons.

Early Signs of Autism

Autism Speaks: Interactive Video Glossary—http://www.autismspeaks.org/what-autism/video-glossary

Centers for Disease Control and Prevention: Autism Spectrum Disorders Signs and Symptoms—http://www.cdc.gov/ncbddd/autism/signs.html

Organizations and Information Resources

American Speech-Language-Hearing Association: Augmentative and Alternative Communication—http://www.asha.org/public/speech/disorders/AAC.htm

The ASHA Leader: Social Communication Strategies for Adolescents With Autism—http://www.asha.org/Publications/leader/2011/110118/Social-Communication-Strategies-for-Adolescents-With-Autism.htm

Autism Institute on Peer Socialization and Play—http://wolfberg.com

Autism Intervention Research Program: Pivotal Response Training—http://www.autismlab.ucsd.edu/about/pivotal-response-training.shtml

Autism Society of America—http://www.autism-society.org

Autism Speaks—http://www.autismspeaks.org

First Signs—http://firstsigns.org

FIRST WORDS Project—http://firstwords.fsu.edu

Social Thinking—http://www.socialthinking.com/

TEACCH Autism Program—http://teacch.com

University of Colorado, Denver: Positive Early Learning Experiences Center—http://www.ucdenver.edu/academics/colleges/SchoolOfEducation/CentersPartnerships/PELE/Pages/PositiveEarlyLearningExperiences.aspx

UCSB Koegel Autism Center—http://www.education.ucsb.edu/autism

Walden Early Childhood Center—http://www.psychiatry.emory.edu/PROGRAMS/autism/Walden.html

Blogs

Autism Blogs Directory—http://autismblogsdirectory.blogspot.com

Applied Behavior Analysis—http://www.appliedbehavioranalysis.blogspot.com

Autism Speaks—http://blog.autismspeaks.org

CARD (Center for Autism and Related Disorders) Community—http://blog.centerforautism.com

A Diary of a Mom—http://adiaryofamom.wordpress.com

The Joy of Autism—http://www.esteeklar.com

Raising a Son With Autism—http://autism--tearsofaclown.blogspot.com

About the Editors

Andrew L. Egel, Ph.D., is professor in the Department of Counseling, Higher Education and Special Education at the University of Maryland. He has developed an ongoing research program in the area of autism while training teachers to work with children and youth with autism spectrum disorders (ASD) and other severe disabilities. Dr. Egel teaches courses in Applied Behavior Analysis (ABA), ASD, and research methodology. His current research interests focus on the development and evaluation of innovative instructional methodologies for use with children with ASD and other severe disabilities. In addition to his research endeavors, Dr. Egel consults with programs involved in the education of children with ASD and other severe disabilities across the country. He also reviews for many leading educational and psychological journals and has made significant contributions in the fields of autism and instructional methodology.

Katherine C. Holman, Ph.D., CCC-SLP, is assistant professor in the Department of Special Education at Towson University and a certified speech-language pathologist. She is the director of the Teacher as Leader in Autism Spectrum Disorder master's program and is a regional autism consultant to the public school system. The focus of her clinical and research work has been on developing effective interventions to improve social connections and communication in young children with autism and strategies for empowering families. She presents nationally and leads seminars for professionals and families on instructional programming to promote successful educational outcomes for individuals with ASD. She has dedicated her life's work to creating a positive influence for and understanding of life on the autism spectrum.

Christine H. Barthold, Ph.D., BCBA-D, is a limited term researcher at the Center for Disabilities Studies, University of Delaware. At the university, she coordinates two federally funded research projects dedicated to understanding how children with autism use symbols to communicate. In addition, she holds a private practice working with young children, adolescents, and adults with autism. The main focus of her clinical work is the use of evidence-based strategies, especially Applied Behavior Analysis (ABA), with children with ASD in the schools. Dr. Barthold consults with school systems across the country in the use of behavioral assessment and intervention methods with children with ASD. She also consults with families in their homes while providing supplementary ABA services.

About the Contributors

Sara Egorin-Hooper has been a special educator in Baltimore County Public Schools (BCPS) for 37 years. She supervises programs for students with ASD and for students with significant cognitive disabilities. Additionally, she adapts curriculum for BCPS to ensure that all students have access to the general education curriculum and to provide teachers with differentiated materials and strategies to support student achievement and success. She also provides professional development to educators and community members.

Paul Livelli, Ph.D., began his career as a one-to-one aide for a student with autism in 1990. Since then he has been a vocational coordinator, special education teacher, and school director for students with ASD in both public and private programs. Currently, Paul has created a program called Mountain Creek Farms in Virginia, where adults with ASD are learning independent living and working skills. He presents at conferences on

educating students with disabilities, while teaching and supervising graduate students at the University of Maryland.

Nicole Pearson is completing her doctorate in school psychology at Fairleigh Dickinson University and pursuing her coursework for board certification in Applied Behavior Analysis. She has trained at Alpine Leaning Group and at the New York Center for Autism Charter School. She is broadly interested in applying effective intervention to children with autism, and in infusing effective ABA techniques into regular education settings. Nicole is currently researching outcomes associated with adaptive behavior measures and peer mentoring programs.

April J. Schwarz, NCSP, has been a school psychologist for the Programs for Students with Autism Spectrum Disorders in Montgomery County Public Schools (MCPS) for 10 years. She conducts assessments for all students in the programs, in addition to providing individual and group counseling for students with Asperger's syndrome. She also provides consultation services on assessment and diagnosis, social skills instruction, and professional development to educators and other school psychologists within the county.

Mary Jane Weiss, Ph.D., BCBA-D, is professor at Endicott College, where she directs the master's program in Applied Behavior Analysis and autism. She previously was Director of Research and Training and Clinical Director of the Douglass Developmental Disabilities Center at Rutgers University for 16 years. Her clinical and research interests center on defining best practice ABA techniques, on evaluating the impact of ABA in learners with autism, and in maximizing family members' expertise and adaptation.